P9-BZZ-254

an imprint of
…unications Ministries
…ngs, CO 80918
…nications, Paris, Ontario
…hmunications, Eastbourne, England

…TATION TO A MEANINGFUL LIFE
…ke Breen and Walt Kallestad

…iters: Adam Palmer, Gayle Smith
…rand Navigation, LLC
…otoDisc

…05
…a
…10 Printing/Year 10 09 08 07 06 05

A PASSIONA

Present

NexGen® is
Cook Comm
Colorado Spr
Cook Commu
Kingsway Cor

GOD'S INVI
© 2005 by Mi

Contributing wr
Cover Design: B
Cover Photo: Ph

First Printing, 20
Printed in Canad
1 2 3 4 5 6 7 8 9

1562927221

A Passionate LIFE

DEVOTIONAL

God's Invitation *to* a Meaningful Life

HONOR **H** BOOKS

Inspiration and Motivation for the Seasons of Life

COOK COMMUNICATIONS MINISTRIES
Colorado Springs, Colorado • Paris, Ontario
KINGSWAY COMMUNICATIONS LTD
Eastbourne, England

INTRODUCTION

We've all received one at some time in our lives. Invitations for weddings, graduations, birthday parties—they all arouse some sort of response in us. It's interesting how our response is usually dictated by who gives the invitation. It seems that the more distant the relationship, the more the invitation seems like an invoice . . . just another present I have to buy. An invitation from a close friend, though, can arouse anticipation. Who else is going to be there? What should I bring? Did you tell them we're coming?

You might have even received an invitation from someone pretty important: the mayor, the pastor, the board president. And this invitation evokes an even different response. Maybe it's a dignified excitement because we've been included in something important. We might even consider some new additions to the wardrobe. It's really true that our response to an invitation depends primarily on who offers it.

God. One short little word elicits more discussion and more controversy than any other uttered by humans. Volumes have been written, wars have been fought, and heroes martyred over what that word means. And in the midst of all of the different explanations for who God is, Christianity occupies a unique place . . . because of an invitation.

Only in Christianity do we meet a God who surveys the landscape of a broken world and rather than waiting for his world to come to him, decides to go to it. Only in Christianity do we encounter a God who chases after humans with a passionate, almost irrational love. Only in Christianity do we meet a God who has planned a way to fix the world of humans, by becoming one. In Jesus, we meet this God who on his own decided to tap us on the shoulder and say, "Can I have this dance?"

And this is the invitation. The God who exists, has entered his broken world in the person of Jesus, and asks, "Will you follow me?"

How will you respond to this invitation? How will I? This is the ultimate question for humanity. Walk with us as we reflect on this invitation, and may we together find this passionate God, inviting us into a passionate life with him.

HOW TO USE THIS DEVOTIONAL

T he devotionals in this journal are all based around the concepts presented in *LifeShapes*. *LifeShapes* takes advantage of our tendency to remember what we see longer than what we hear. Biblical principles connected to basic shapes help you remember how to follow Jesus' example in every aspect of your life. As you read these devotionals, notice that we have connected each to one of the following *LifeShapes*.

The Circle: Jesus marked the beginning of his ministry by calling on all believers to *repent* and *believe* (Mark 1:15). The Circle takes us through the process of repentance and belief and faith so that our lives can be fully changed for Christ.

The Semi-Circle: Every day, week, month, and year of Jesus' ministry was marked by periods of work and rest. He calls upon us to find the same rhythms of fruitfulness and abiding characterized by equal moments of work and rest in our lives (John 15:1-4).

The Triangle: Jesus had the perfect balance in all the relationships of his life, UP with the Father, IN with the disciples, and OUT with the rest of the world. We can live a balanced and relational life by following the same example of Jesus seen in Matthew 9:35-38.

The Square: Jesus is greatest leader of all time. And the fact that we all have at least one other person looking to us as an example makes us leaders as well. Use Jesus' example to teach you the four principles of good leadership and personal growth (Mark 1:16-20; Luke 12:32-34; John 15:14-15; Matt. 28:18-20).

The Pentagon: Ephesians 4 tells of the five ministry gifts we have all been granted at least one of which. Once you discover what God designed you for, you can stop striving to be something you weren't meant to be and do something that will truly build up the body of Christ.

The Hexagon: Jesus taught us the perfect prayer in Matthew 6:9-13. Learn the six phrases that Jesus prayed and what he truly meant by them and your prayer life will become the most effective and dynamic you've ever experienced.

The Heptagon: Biological life has seven basic requirements and our spiritual lives have the same. Practice each of them and your spirit will be renewed and refreshed with the presence of God (1 Pet. 2:4-5).

The Octagon: Evangelism can be a scary thing for those who aren't really sure what they're doing. But Jesus simply tells us to be on the lookout for the *Person of Peace* (Luke 10:5-6). Understanding this concept makes evangelism and discipleship a much simpler task.

For more information on *LifeShapes* and other products available, visit **www.LifeShapes.com**.

GOD'S INVITATION

I f you're reading this devotional, then most likely you desire to connect with God. And if you're like most people who want to connect with God, you've found this desire to be a little tricky. We want to find God, but we wonder if he really wants to be found. Prayer can feel like a monologue to an empty room. Or to Someone who's far too important or preoccupied to spend time with us. So we keep trying. And in the middle of our gyrations to find God, in Genesis 3 we hear him walking in the cool of day, calling to us, "Where are you?"

> **Then the man and his wife heard the sound of the LORD God as he was walking in the garden in the cool of the day, and they hid from the LORD God among the trees of the garden. But the LORD God called to the man, "Where are you?"**
>
> GENESIS 3:8-9

It's almost impossible to believe that this God who created everything that exists could casually and comfortably stroll through a garden on this little earth. And even more unbelievable is that he would invite us to stroll with him. Yet he does. Here in Genesis 3 we see the picture of the way life is "supposed to be." God isn't asking how your devotions went today. He isn't asking how productive you were today. He simply asks, "Where are you?" God just wants to be with you. And to make it even better, he's coming to find you. He's not sitting and waiting in quiet frustration for you to find him. He's looking for you. Just YOU. Have you ever taken a walk on a cool summer night with someone you love? Have you ever noticed that there are just some things you don't talk about? You don't talk about work. You don't talk about your ambitions. You don't try to impress your companion on the journey. It would spoil it. You might not even talk at all. You just take it in. You just be.

THE
TRIANGLE

UP

And so here is the invitation God extends to you: "I'm taking a walk. Would you like to come?"

> *God, I would like to walk with you like I read about in this passage. It sounds really good. But for some reason, I have a hard time believing that you just want to be with me. I feel the need to impress you, to appease you, or to convince you I'm worth spending time with. Help me believe that you're the one inviting me, and that just plain, old me is what you really want. Amen.*

RIDE OF YOUR LIFE

Jake and Louisa were having fun at the theme park that day. From the moment they'd arrived, the park's centerpiece—a winding, twisting, steel roller coaster—had been calling Louisa's name. They'd ridden a few other, smaller rides, had some overpriced lunch, and let it settle while cooling off on the water ride. Now Louisa was ready to heed the big coaster's call. Grabbing Jake's hand, she dragged him toward the steel monster, but he held back. Louisa pleaded with him to go, but he refused. So she went by herself. And loved it! As Jake watched, he began to notice how often the ride was running. While it looked risky from down below, he saw that it actually was quite safe. It ran once a minute, all day long—every day of the theme park's entire season. Maybe I should've gone on that ride, Jake said to himself. Finally, Louisa came back, smiling widely, telling him how great the coaster was. She was ready to go again. This time Jake submitted . . . and had the time of his life.

The moment they saw him they worshipped him.
Some, though, held back, not sure about *worship*,
about risking themselves totally.

MATTHEW 28:17 (MSG)

Jesus is inviting us into the worship of him, into the greatest ride of our lives. He's imploring us to jump on. Ride in the front car. It's worth the wait. And while it might be risky, as long as we stick with him, we're perfectly safe. And thrilled! It's worth throwing ourselves into with abandon. It's worth the risk.

THE
TRIANGLE

UP

Jesus is inviting you to risk yourself totally in worshipping him. Will you?

Jesus, I have to say, I like the sound of this. Even though I may not be much of a risk-taker, I'm thinking that maybe it's time to climb aboard this great ride with you. I thank you that as I go through the many spirals and loops of life, that you're right there with me. What a great ride you offer, help me to climb on board. Amen.

"WHERE ARE YOU?"

Bobby had a particularly unsavory babysitter. Not that there was really anything wrong with her. It was just that for some unknown reason Bobby, the 5 year old, decided he didn't like her. So he resolved to escape from the house so as to avoid further contact with his nemesis. He managed to tear a hole in the screen of the front door and climb through the opening. Freedom! He ran outside and was exhilarated with the success of his escape. But shortly after his celebration, it dawned on him what he had done. He imagined the kind of reaction his parents would have upon news of his escape and the demolished screen door. This was not good. So Bobby did the logical thing that any kid in his situation would do. He hid in the garage.

> Then the man and his wife heard the sound of the
> LORD God as he was walking in the garden in the cool
> of the day, and they hid from the LORD God among
> the trees of the garden. But the LORD God
> called to the man, "Where are you?"
> He answered, "I heard you in the garden,
> and I was afraid because I was naked; so I hid."
>
> GENESIS 3:8-10

Really this is the kind of thing we continue to do all the way into our elderly years. When we're not proud of our behavior, rarely do we choose to share it with as many people as we can. Instead, we hide. Shame makes us hide. Adam and Eve got the distinction of being the first people to experience shame, and they hid. Something that is amazing about their story, however, is that when God came to find Adam and Eve, he already knew that they had disobeyed him. Yet he came to look for them anyway. Even when his kids are disobedient, God wants to be with us. He just wants us to come out of hiding. That doesn't mean he'll look the other way when we sin! We still need to repent and ask him to forgive us. And because Jesus went to the cross . . . we can. And he does.

THE
CIRCLE

REPENT

Jesus invites you to come out of hiding. Will you?

Jesus, I do things almost every day that I'm not proud of. My attitudes, thoughts, and even actions can be embarrassing to recount to anyone—especially you. Help me to believe that you still love me even when you need to correct me. Help me to come out of hiding. Amen.

A RICHER LIFE

Remember your first day of school? It wasn't that big of a deal a few years ago, but now with the sudden proliferation of video cameras and fancy digital still cameras, the first day of school is a production to be recorded and viewed ad infinitum. In a simpler time, the first day of school carried more emotional weight. The first day of school meant boarding the bus for the first time, or being dropped off in front of the school for the first time ever. Remember the trepidation you felt at leaving your parents behind for this new mission of life? Remember the exhilaration you felt, stepping into the unexplored territory of kindergarten? Remember how that exhilaration outweighed your fears? Yes, it was a little scary, but there were all these other kids! And paste! And construction paper! And that really nice teacher! It was a kid-themed wonderland.

> Going on from there, he saw two other brothers, James son of Zebedee and his brother John. They were in a boat with their father Zebedee, preparing their nets. Jesus called them, and immediately they left the boat and their father and followed him.
>
> MATTHEW 4:21-22

When Jesus invited James and John to come with him, they had to choose to leave their father behind. Fortunately for them, the exhilaration outweighed the trepidation and they immediately left their boat. Being in the boat with their father, they were practicing the family trade. They were living their normal lives. They were doing something they thought they'd do for the rest of their lives. They were settled. Secure. Safe. But Jesus invited them into a new phase of their lives—one they didn't know would even be there. And they took him up on it.

THE
SQUARE

D 1

Jesus is inviting you to leave the security and safety of all you know and live a life that's made richer by following him. Will you leave your comforts behind and do it?

Jesus, like a child on the first day of school, I'm excited about what's in store for me. What you've planned for me. But leaving my comforts behind, my security behind . . . well, that's a little scary. Help me to feel the exhilaration that comes with following you. Help me to let go. I love you, Jesus. Amen.

HOME SWEET HOME

M ost of us have had the pleasure and/or misfortune of being the guest at someone's home. Staying at someone else's house always has its oddities: the way the house smells, where the bathroom is located, the sounds at night, the temperature, the pets. And no matter how well you know the host, it just never seems like you can be at ease like you would be at your own home. Should you leave the hallway light on? Can you leave the toiletries out on the counter? Even if you had a great time while being a guest, there's just nothing better than coming home. Home is where you can leave your toothpaste out on the counter. Home is where you can let your guard down. Home is where you can be yourself. And so God invites us home. A place where there is "breathing room, a place to get away from it all."

> You've always given me breathing room, a place to get
> away from it all, A lifetime pass to your safe-house,
> an open invitation as your guest. You've always
> taken me seriously, God, made me welcome among
> those who know and love you.
>
> PSALM 61:3-5 (MSG)

God invites us to a home that isn't limited to geography. This is the true home for your soul where you can find rest, peace, sanity. It's amazing that the stress, pressure, and noise of life can so bombard us that we can come to feel like strangers in our own home. It can even get to where we feel like strangers in our own skin. Yet God invites us: "Come home." Come home to the One who created the concept of home. Come home to him who is home. Come home to where you can truly be yourself, in the presence of the One that created you and loves you infinitely, right now. Come home.

THE
SEMI-
CIRCLE

And so hear the invitation from God: "Will you come home?"

God, this sounds great. I'd like to come home. I do sometimes feel like a stranger in my own skin. Life just demands so much. So I'm coming home. I accept your invitation. Amen.

A LIFE OF LOVE

How many steps an hour do you suppose Jesus took? The Bible says he went throughout Galilee, teaching, preaching, and healing. How long do you figure that took him? We can imagine that Jesus had to wade through crowds and crowds of people as he went about his mission here on earth. The news about the healings he performed went all over the region, and people began to seek him out, desperately, hoping he could help them. People in pain. People who were sick. People possessed by demons. People who couldn't walk. All sorts of people approached Jesus. And he touched them. He reached them. He preached to them. He loved them . . . and he gave them hope. The hope of God's kingdom. The hope of freedom.

> Jesus went throughout Galilee, teaching in their synagogues, preaching the good news of the kingdom, and healing every disease and sickness among the people.
> News about him spread all over Syria, and people brought to him all who were ill with various diseases, those suffering severe pain, the demon-possessed, those having seizures, and the paralyzed, and he healed them.
>
> MATTHEW 4:23-24

Now Jesus has called us to be his hands and feet. To walk among the people; to reach out to them and touch them. To love them. To offer them the hope they so desperately need but are unaware of. Jesus healed people while he was here, and we're called to do the same. We're called to heal broken hearts. To heal wounded souls. To heal shattered spirits. Jesus is inviting us to join him on this healing mission. He's inviting us to love other people, and in so doing, heal them. His every move on earth was motivated by love; our every move should be the same.

THE
TRIANGLE

IN

Jesus is inviting you to heal people by loving them in whatever way they need. Are you up to it?

Dear Jesus, I want to live a passionate life. A life of loving people, just like you did. Of providing what they need: a shoulder to cry on, a listening ear, a ride to work, a few bucks for lunch. Whatever, Jesus. I want to be an instrument of your healing in this world. Amen.

SHARE THE NEWS

Have you ever had really good news you wanted to tell the world about—something like an engagement or birth announcement? News like that is hard to keep in. We want to blab about it to just about everyone—especially people who know us well. Good news brings happiness and we want those we care about to share in our happiness. But what makes it even more fun is to break the news with someone else who already knows it. So the prospective couple visits a relative together to tell of their engagement. The husband accompanies the wife to her parents' house to be there when they first see the ultrasound photo of the grandchild they didn't know was there. Being able to deliver good news together enhances the experience of it.

> Then Jesus came to them and said, "All authority in heaven and on earth has been given to me. Therefore go and make disciples of all nations, baptizing them in the name of the Father and of the Son and of the Holy Spirit, and teaching them to obey everything I have commanded you. And surely I am with you always, to the very end of the age."
>
> MATTHEW 28:18-20

It's amazing how hard we will work for things we don't really want. And in the face of our muddled behavior, God makes an unbelievable invitation, unbelievable in the literal sense of the world. Can I really believe that I can be completely satisfied by something I pay nothing for? Everybody knows there are no "free lunches." And nobody wants to be a charity case. Besides, charity cases only get the leftovers. If you want the best, you have to work for it. But God persists. "Come buy . . . without money. Why spend your labor on what does not satisfy?" Something about God's offer offends our sense of fairness. People should be responsible and work for their rewards. But God offers us that which no money can buy, and nobody deserves: himself.

THE
HEPTAGON

NUTRITION

So God invites us, come be satisfied, at no cost. Will you come?

God, I do want to be satisfied. But when I know that I can't earn it, it means I can't control what I get. And I wonder if you really will give me what you're offering. Help me to relax and trust you. Come and fill me up. Amen.

ANOTHER CHANCE

Ah, the "do-over . . ." That wonderful childhood rule that lets you roll again when the dice accidentally fall off the board, that lets you re-play the down because the tree got in your way, that lets you hide again because Jimmy totally peeked while he was counting. Sadly, we don't get the do-over much once we've grown up. If we say something stupid, hurtful, or mean in the midst of an argument, the damage is done. If the boss overhears us making fun of him, the damage is done. If we lose our temper and scream at our children, the damage is done. We all make mistakes, and we all need a do-over at some point. Jesus is inviting us to accept one from him, because we've all been afflicted with an ugly, deforming disease called sin.

> **While Jesus was in one of the towns, a man came along**
> **who was covered with leprosy. When he saw Jesus,**
> **he fell with his face to the ground and begged him,**
> **"Lord, if you are willing, you can make me clean."**
>
> LUKE 5:12

Much like this man's leprosy, our sin covers us and makes us unworthy. But when we fall at Jesus' feet, and say, "Lord, if you're willing, make me clean," we're accepting Jesus' offer. He is willing. He will make us clean. He will give us the do-over we so desperately need. But not before we ask him for it. Not before we humble ourselves, recognize our leprous condition, and fall facedown before him. The man in this passage begged Jesus to make him clean. Our sin is a burden we needn't bear. We should feel passionate about accepting Jesus' offer of a do-over.

THE
CIRCLE

BELIEVE

The hand has been extended. Jesus is inviting you to accept his cleansing. Do you want a do-over?

Jesus, I know I can't change the past. I know I can't literally do something over. But I also know that when I let you change me, my old self, the self that messes up, gets a little bit smaller. I accept your offer of a do-over, Lord. I know you're willing; please make me clean. Amen.

THE FIRE OF GOD

Have you ever sat next to a campfire and just watched it burn? It's amazing how mesmerizing it can be. The fire is warm and comforting, a pool of light in a dark night. People gather around it and feel safe. Yet at the very same time, it's dangerous. If we get too close, we feel the searing heat on our faces and back away. And anything that gets thrown into the fire is much consumed in short order. In fact, it's really hard to describe exactly what fire is. It's actually much easier to describe fire by what it does. Whatever the case, everything that fire touches is changed.

> "I'm baptizing you here in the river, turning your old
> life in for a kingdom life. The real action comes next:
> The main character in this drama—compared to him
> I'm a mere stagehand—will ignite the kingdom life
> within you, a fire within you, the Holy Spirit
> within you, changing you from the inside out.
> He's going to clean house—make a clean sweep
> of your lives. He'll place everything true in
> its proper place before God; everything false
> he'll put out with the trash to be burned."
>
> MATT. 3:11-12 (MSG)

John the Baptist equates God's presence in us with fire. Now Jesus is inviting us to a life, a passionate life, which is "a fire within you, the Holy Spirit within you, changing you from the inside out." God's presence in us can be a source of sustenance and security in the midst of a dark and cold world. But at the very same time, God's presence in us is dangerous, untamable, and all-consuming. In our very safe culture of automated seat belts, biking helmets, and touchless no-germ faucets, we run the serious risk of forgetting that

THE
CIRCLE

God is not safe. The God who made daisies and daffodils is the same God who made ear-splitting thunder and crushing ocean breakers. And fire. God's invitation to us is to let him into our lives, to dwell with us and give us his warmth, comfort, and safety. And to demand everything of us, to change everything he touches and consume all that is not like him.

And so the invitation stands: Will you let me burn within you?

God, I'm stirred, and scared, by the thought of you being a fire within me. I want to have passion, but be safe at the same time. I want you to burn inside of me, but I'm afraid of being burned. Help me, God, to trust you, and let you burn in me both for my safety and for my transformation. Amen.

GET REAL

E ver felt like an outsider? Who hasn't? The person who doesn't quite fit in with the rest of the crowd. The one kid in school who sits alone in the lunchroom. The office reject, who has no one to discuss anything with while standing at the water cooler or coffee pot. Countless movies have featured characters that stand in the wings while the "insiders" cavort on the stage of life for all to see. These characters and movies are successful because they tap into a deep urge inside all of us to be wanted. In some form or fashion, whether we admit it or not, we want to be wanted. We want to be a part of the group. We want to be insiders.

> **"I'm here inviting outsiders, not insiders—an invitation**
> **to a changed life, changed inside and out."**
> LUKE 5:32 (MSG)

Jesus ignores the performances of the insiders and looks to the wings, seeking us out. He doesn't want showboats; he wants authentic people who aren't afraid to be real with him, to admit they're on the outside instead of covering up their insecurities with performance. He wants the people who realize all of us are outsiders. And then he wants to invite us to a changed life. He wants to change us, inside and out, so that we become a part of his crowd. Part of his play. People who will showcase their change and invite others to join in.

THE
CIRCLE

REPENT

Jesus is inviting you to have a changed life. Will you accept?

O Jesus, I'm so tired of pretending like I have it all together. I'm so tired of pretending like I'm with the insiders, even though I know, in my heart of hearts, I'm not. I pray that you'll change me inside and out; help me to realize my outsider status. I accept your invitation, and in turn, I invite you in. Amen.

REPENT AND BELIEVE

"**T**he Kingdom of heaven is near." For the first-
century Jew, this statement aroused much emotion
and expectation. The modern equivalent of the anticipation
they might have felt would be if we got a phone call that
said, "The President of the United States is coming to your
neighborhood." Can you imagine how you would feel after
hearing that? The President is coming to my neighborhood?
What have we done to deserve such an honor? But to this
exciting announcement Jesus adds one little word that sends
it an unexpected direction: Repent.

> **From that time on Jesus began to preach,**
> **"Repent, for the kingdom of heaven is near."**
> MATTHEW 4:17

Just one little word takes this statement from heady exhilaration to an embarrassing assessment. The President is coming, but you need to change yourself if you want to see him.
What? I'm a good citizen! But just like the Jews of Jesus'
time, we expect someone that is much different than the one
who actually comes. When we hear the King is coming, we
want to share in his power. Yet he gave it up. We want to
gain recognition by being associated with him. He accepted

none. We want influence. He gave it away. The doorway to God's kingdom is repentance. For the King to associate with you, you must humble yourself the same way he did, " . . . Who, being in very nature God, did not consider equality with God something to be grasped, but made himself nothing, taking the very nature of a servant" (Phil. 2:6-7). Everybody wants to be the friend of the King. We all want to be identified with greatness. Yet the big surprise of the universe is that our natural inclinations for being with the King are all wrong. To be with the King, we need to change. We need to repent.

THE CIRCLE

So Jesus extends his invitation to you: I want to be with you. Will you repent?

Jesus, I believe you really are the King of the universe. And I want you to be with me, to visit my home and associate with me. But I admit that it's often for the wrong reasons. I confess my desires for recognition, power, and influence. And I ask you to help me to change. I repent. Amen.

31

EXPECT NOTHING

E ver had someone compliment you on something in the
hopes that you'll return the favor? "That's an awesome
shirt," they say, hoping to hear you comment on the
awesomeness of their shirt, which they just got for their
birthday. "You did a great job during the presentation,"
they'll offer up after a business meeting, hoping to get some
encouragement from you about their portion of the presentation. They're doing something that's basically good, but their
motivation isn't pure. They're giving in order to get.

> **Then Jesus said to his host, "When you give a luncheon
> or dinner, do not invite your friends, your brothers or
> relatives, or your rich neighbors; if you do, they may
> invite you back and so you will be repaid."**
>
> LUKE 14:12

In the example Jesus gives in today's passage of Scripture,
we're not supposed to give something in the hopes of getting
something. We know God sees our actions and will reward
us in due time, and that should be good enough for us. Jesus
is inviting us to give of ourselves without expecting anything
in return. He wants us to give to others simply for the sake

of giving. Because he is our reward. Jesus never wants us to waste our time seeking the praise of the world. He didn't do it himself. Jesus simply wants us to give of ourselves without any assurance that the people we give to will accept our gift. It is the giving he is concerned with; the reward will come.

Will you give without expecting anything in return?

THE
HEXAGON

THE
FATHER'S
PROVISION

Jesus, thank you for being a great role model for giving. You gave it all, Jesus. I pray that you'll help me to be like you. Help me to give my all. Amen.

FISHERS OF MEN

Have you ever heard of an offer that was "too good to be true?" In our over-sold consumer culture, we hear invitations like "buy now," "while supplies last," and "limited time only" that all promise the deal of a lifetime if we'll only act now. But most of us have learned to be skeptical of offers such as these, and for good reason.

> **Walking along the beach of Lake Galilee,**
> **Jesus saw two brothers: Simon (later called Peter) and**
> **Andrew. They were fishing, throwing their nets into the**
> **lake. It was their regular work. Jesus said to them,**
> **"Come with me. I'll make a new kind of fisherman out**
> **of you. I'll show you how to catch men and women**
> **instead of perch and bass." They didn't ask questions,**
> **but simply dropped their nets and followed.**
> MATTHEW 4:18-20 (MSG)

Rarely do high-pressure sales offers deliver on their promises. There are always a few more items in the back of the store. Or if you do buy the last one, now that you have it you realize it's good that there weren't any more of them. So it's almost hard to believe that when Jesus came to Peter and Andrew, all he had to say to get them to leave their jobs, on the spot, was "Come with me." What was so compelling about Jesus' invitation that they could leave their sole source of income and risk everything they had all in a moment's notice? Maybe they had heard about Jesus' baptism and the rumors that God's audible voice had been heard, identifying Jesus as God's chosen One. Maybe they had been overcome by Jesus' simple yet direct proclamation, "Repent, for the kingdom of heaven is near." (Matt. 4:17) Perhaps they had heard him teach and saw this as their chance to become a distinguished pupil, respected and revered. Maybe it was just a penetrating look from Jesus that made them do it. Whatever it was, they did it. So what are you going to do? He is making the same invitation to you. Jesus has directed his attention toward you and said, "Come with me." Will you ask questions before coming? Will you ask for some time to think about it? Will you send him to voicemail? Or will you drop what you're doing and follow him?

THE
SQUARE

Jesus invites you, "Come with me." What will you do?

Jesus, I want to hear your invitation the same way that Peter and Andrew did. I want to hear what they heard and follow you without questions or hesitation. Help me to hear your invitation to come. Jesus, I will follow you. Amen.

LOVING WITH GRACE

A aron stood on the corner in downtown, waiting as the ministry team he was traveling with went inside the run-down hotel. It was a rough part of town, and the hotel was one of the roughest spots. It was so dangerous, they only allowed two trusted members of the ministry team inside, and the rest had to wait on the corner. A man crossed the busy downtown street to approach the group. "You guys handing out food today?" "Not right now. Later." Aaron struck up a conversation with the man, who was clearly drunk. "You can get out of here, you know. You don't have to live like this." "How?" the man said. Aaron told the man about the ministry team. "We have a place where you can live for free. Get off the street. Learn a skill. Earn your living." "No thanks," the man replied. "When will you be handing out the food?"

> **"But when you give a banquet, invite the poor, the
> crippled, the lame, the blind, and you will be blessed.
> Although they cannot repay you, you will be repaid
> at the resurrection of the righteous."**
>
> LUKE 14:13-14

The man Aaron spoke to wasn't the first to turn down his offer of help. But at least Aaron had been able to extend the offer. Jesus wants us to make that offer, too. He's invited us to love the unlovable with him, even if we experience the frustration and hurt that comes with their rejection. He said to invite the poor, the crippled, the lame, and the blind to our banquet. Not just the physically homeless, but the spiritually homeless. Whether they accept the invitation is up to them, but they must be invited. And we are the ones to do that.

THE
OCTAGON

PERSON
OF
PEACE

Will you invite them? Will you extend a hand and love the unlovable?

Jesus, thank you for inviting me to your banquet while I was unlovable. I accept this mission, Jesus. I accept your challenge to invite the unlovable. I know it'll be hard, so I pray you'll give me compassion and boldness. Help me to see everyone the way you see them. Amen.

YOU DO IT

E ver seen a five-year-old boy help his dad mow the lawn?
Now, mind you, he's not really doing any mowing.
Rather, he's pushing his plastic toy lawnmower behind as
Dad cuts the grass with the real lawnmower. But he enjoys
it, and Dad loves his company. One day the boy demands
that he do the real mowing himself. Dad gives him a shot
at it. He struggles to understand how to put gasoline in the
mower. His plump little arms strain just trying to get the
mower to start. After a few unsuccessful attempts at pulling
the cord, he steps back and says, "Here you go, Dad. You
do it."

You're blessed when you're at the end of your rope.
With less of you there is more of God and his rule.
MATTHEW 5:3 (MSG)

Most of us at some point in our journey with God uncon-
sciously develop an "I-can-take-it-from-here" attitude. Often
times out of good motives, we want to live life as if God only
needed to give us a jumpstart, but we can handle the rest on
our own. And some of us even feel like that's what God is

expecting. But just like the five-year-old boy and the lawn-mower, the reality is that we never have been living life on our own. God is the one who has been doing the "real" life out in front of us. Jesus invites us to live in the constant reality that we're incapable of doing life on our own. To be at the "end of your rope" is to face reality honestly. We cannot live life without God's constant leading, support, and intervention.

THE
SQUARE

D 2

So the invitation stands: Will you let me help you?

God, I often feel like I need to prove something to you. Thanks for the times that you allow me to see that I can't make it without you. God, help me to let you help me. Amen.

HOPE IN LOSS

P retty much all loss stinks. The loss of body fat may be the only welcome loss out there. Other than that, it's just no fun. But life is full of it, and it leaves us with a persistent, painful sense of unchangeable absence. Regret, anger, and guilt are all common companions of loss. Loss can feel like failure, even when we had no control over what happened. And in a culture where winning is everything, loss can even become a stigma . . . a label synonymous with "undesirable." We often call the repeat offenders "losers."

> **"You're blessed when you feel you've lost what
> is most dear to you. Only then can you be
> embraced by the One most dear to you."**
> MATTHEW 5:4 (MSG)

What's so great about Jesus is that he never sidestepped or minimized the harsh realities of life. Rather, he faced them head on and, more than simply faced them, he reinterpreted them. Jesus understands that in life on earth, at some point you're bound to lose. No matter how successful or hardworking you may be, eventually you'll experience failure. No matter how much you attempt to control your world, something will eventually get out of control. It's inevitable, because we're not God. Jesus invites us not to escape from the difficulty of loss, but rather to embrace it. This approach would be masochistic were it not for the paradoxical reality that our loss can make space for God. A loving father never wants his children to get sick. But that same loving father isn't entirely disappointed when his children want to just cuddle with him for long periods of time because they don't feel well. God knows we need him. And he knows that loss is a part of life. So he invites us to take our loss to him, and let him fill it.

THE
CIRCLE

KAIROS

God invites you to invite him into your loss. Will you?

God, it's hard for me to believe that some of the losses I've experienced could ever be filled. But I want to give you a chance. Come into the absence that loss has created in my life, and make it full again. Amen.

STAY AT MY PLACE

We've all had experiences where people we didn't necessarily like to spend time with have ingratiated themselves into our lives, inviting themselves along on a lunch outing or to a party or some other place we really don't care to interact with them. Jesus' invitation to Zacchaeus is the opposite of that. This is like your hero—your personal favorite athlete or actor or politician or writer or musician or whatever—inviting themselves over to your house for the evening. "Got a comfy couch? I'm spending the night!" And even that pales in comparison, because this isn't an athlete or actor or musician. This is Jesus. The One everyone's talking about! The guy you climbed up a tree to get a glimpse of! And he's asking—no, telling—you about coming to your house. Your house!

> **When Jesus reached the spot, he looked up and said**
> **to him, "Zacchaeus, come down immediately. I**
> **must stay at your house today."**
> LUKE 19:5

What an unbelievable experience, having someone of that stature inviting himself to come crash at your place for the night. How humbling that must've been for Zacchaeus.

How humbling it must be for us, when we realize that Jesus is inviting himself into our spiritual homes. He stands at the door, knocking. He wants to come in. He wants to test out the couch, see what we cook up for dinner, engage in some late-night conversation. And best of all, he doesn't care how clean the place is! Because when he stays with us, our lives are changed for good. Zacchaeus had been involved in some shady dealings, but after his encounter with Jesus, he refunded all the money he'd stolen. He changed. The same goes for us.

THE HEPTAGON MOVEMENT

Jesus is inviting himself into your house. Will you let him in?

Jesus, I'll be honest with you. My house isn't the tidiest right now. There's some dirt in the corners and some cobwebs I haven't really dealt with. There's a mess in the kitchen, and it's been a while since I washed my dirty laundry. But I'm thankful that I don't have to clean up before you can come in. You just want to be with me. You can overlook the messes, and even help me take care of them. I invite you into my home. Change me, Lord. Amen.

YOU HAVE IT ALL

D o you remember Christmas as a kid? The anticipation of a full day of nothing but presents makes the average kid wild with excitement. Visions of DVDs and X-boxes dance in the heads of millions of kids around the world the night before Christmas. And then Christmas day comes, and the living room is littered with torn wrapping paper, boxes, and instructions. The kids are finally playing with their long-awaited toys. That night before bedtime, the new toys are given a special place in the bedroom while the old toys are packed away. But as the days wear on, the novelty of the new gifts begins to fade.

> **You're blessed when you're content with just who you are—no more, no less. That's the moment you find yourselves proud owners of everything that can't be bought.**
> MATTHEW 5:5 (MSG)

Eventually, new toys begin to take on the same status as the old. And kids begin to long for the next Christmas, when their true desires can be met with the latest toy on the market. And the truth is we never really grow out of it. The toys just change. A new house, a new job, another career move, a new church. All make the same promises as the new toy. But all of them eventually fade and leave us wanting something different, something more. In the middle of this endless cycle of desire and disappointment, Jesus extends to us a radical invitation. Get off of the carousel. Leave it behind. We are invited to want nothing. Be content with the simplicity of who you are. Be content with what God has given you: himself.

THE
PENTAGON

Jesus extends to you this invitation: Be content. Can you trust me?

Jesus, I do want to be content, but it's hard for me to believe that where I'm at right now is somewhere I can be content. Or even want to. Yet I want to be free from the constant cycle of desire and disappointment. Help me. I want to be free to be content. Amen.

JUST BE YOURSELF

There's a trend lately among young fashionable women to wear rings topped with what look like enormous gems harvested from some sort of pirate treasure chest. But these pieces are far from being the real thing. They're phony—nothing more than smartly cut pieces of glass.

> He went on to tell a story to the guests around the table. Noticing how each had tried to elbow into the place of honor, he said "When someone invites you to dinner, don't take the place of honor. Somebody more important than you might have been invited by the host. Then he'll come and call out in front of every-body, "You're in the wrong place. The place of honor belongs to this man." Red-faced, you'll have to make your way to the very last table, the only place left. When you're invited to dinner, go and sit at the last place. Then when the host comes he may very well say, "Friend, come up to the front." That will give the din-ner guests something to talk about! What I'm saying is, If you walk around with your nose in the air, you're going to end up flat on your face. But if you're content to be simply yourself, you will become more than yourself.
>
> LUKE 14:7-11 (MSG)

STANDING FIRM

ompetitive but friendly, Lisa was an athlete at heart. She loved playing recreational sports, especially with big group of friends. And every summer when the ather was warm enough, she and her friends loved to to the park and play volleyball. Sand volleyball. Lisa ed the feeling of stepping onto the hot sand on top, n burrowing her toes down into it to find the cool layer lerneath. She loved the roughness against the arches of bare feet as she chased down a high lob from the other n. She enjoyed the camaraderie that came from a game played, even if her team lost. But after a few rounds on t sand, her teammates changed their collective minds and ted campaigning to stand on solid ground.

**So, friends, confirm God's invitation to you,
his choice of you. Don't put it off; do it now.
Do this, and you'll have your life on a firm footing.**

2 PETER 1:10 (MSG)

Vhile "beach" volleyball was fun for a short time, nately the unstable playing surface couldn't compare to irmness of solid ground. The solid ground soothed tired

Even the smallest diamond ring—the real thing—is worth much more than the glass alternative. It is what it is, and it doesn't need to show itself off. It just remains a diamond. Because we value diamonds, they are worth more than any rock or piece of glass. But how tempting it is for us to act like something we are not. How tempting it is to pretend we are the enormous piece of ice on someone's ring finger. "I am important!" you want to scream. "I should be honored!" That inclination is something Jesus tells us to avoid. Instead, we just need to be who we are. Be yourself. Putting on airs for the sake of others will always lead to eventual humiliation, but if you accept yourself as the diamond you are, you become more than just a diamond. You are valuable.

THE
CIRCLE

What do you think? Can you be yourself?

Jesus, this sounds kind of selfish to me, but I want to be an authentic Christian. I want people to know that I am honest about who I am. Honest about my failings. Honest about my own worth. I want you to be the one who exalts me; I'm tired of exalting myself. Help me to be myself, Jesus—the person you created me to be. Amen.

GOD, I'M HUNGRY

Have you ever traveled to a foreign country? If you
have, you already know the excitement of entering
into a strange land where the sights are unfamiliar and the
people speak a different language. The smells, the sounds,
the homes . . . everything is new and different. For some,
adjusting to a new culture is a thrill. For others, it's a panic.
Either way, one of the biggest adjustments to foreign travel is
the food. Everyone has to eat. But not everyone has the same
taste. Some travelers try whatever unidentifiable delicacy is
offered them. And there are those who are more conservative, preferring to stick to foods identified only by golden
arches.

> **You're blessed when you've worked up**
> **a good appetite for God. He's food and drink**
> **in the best meal you'll ever eat.**
> MATTHEW 5:6 (MSG)

No matter how adventurous or conservative you may be,
at some point when traveling overseas, you begin craving
familiar foods. You start reliving fond memories of Mom's
cooking or your favorite late-night snacks. The longer you

stay abroad, the more frequently your mind stray
thoughts about the food at home. It becomes a
of nostalgia and fraternity with your fellow trave
And then—finally—the moment
comes. You get off of the airplane on
your home soil, and make your way
to the nearest restaurant you can find.
Your beam at the waitress as you
make your order of "real" food. And
as your plate comes you smell the
wholesome goodness of food from
home. Jesus invites us to this very meal. Here
Earth, we are travelers on foreign soil. All kind
offered to us daily—accomplishment, recogni
popularity. But none of these ever really satisfy
the food of our true home where our Father li
says, come home. Come to the place where he
meal, where his body and his blood are the su
will satisfy us for eternity.

Jesus invites you to dinner. Will you come

HE

NU

God, I really do want to be satisfied. I
to eat the food that not only satisfies m
what I need. Will you help me to belie
you're what I want. Thanks. Amen.

calf muscles, now aching from overworking themselves on the shifting sand. It brought relief to the upper body, which was now back to its normal way of maintaining balance. It brought comfort to strained feet, giving them unmoving support. Life is far from a game, but God does invite us to enjoy it on the firm footing he provides. He's invited us to step off the irritating, ever-shifting sands and onto a foundation that never moves. He saw us on the sand, hurting and exhausted, and reached out his hand to pull us onto the solid ground he provides.

THE
TRIANGLE

UP

God is inviting you to stand with him on firm footing. Will you take the step?

Jesus, I love you. I thank you for your kindness toward me. I thank you that you see the need I have to stand firm, to stand with you. Thank you for inviting me to solid ground. I want to stand with you. I want that firm footing. Amen.

TAKE A STAND

We live in a country where popular opinion actually determines the leaders of a nation. Election time in America is a phenomenon; millions of dollars are spent and brilliant strategists plot to sway the opinions of millions of voters toward their candidate. And this dynamic spills into most other areas of life in America as well. Mass media has created a "pop culture," which by its very definition supposedly represents the majority opinion of the entire nation. Popular culture defines acceptable social practices and fashions. It even identifies the prevailing ideologies of the day.

> **"Stand up for me against world opinion and I'll stand up for you before my Father in heaven. If you turn tail and run, do you think I'll cover for you?"**
> MATTHEW 10:32-33 (MSG)

America defines its leadership, social relationships, and thought structures by what is popular. And in the middle of all of this, Jesus invites us to an exceedingly counter-cultural challenge: Stand up for me against world opinion. This is a tough challenge, because most of us who grew up in America have learned from the sixth grade on that to go against what is popular is to invite ridicule and isolation. Each generation has a different name for those who don't catch on to the cultural norms: dorks, geeks, nerds, losers, freaks. Whatever the title your generation used, the results are the same. Go against what is accepted, and you're out. Jesus' challenge is a hard one. But Jesus knows all about the price of going against the grain. And he offers us this comfort with the invitation: Stand up for me, and I'll stand up for you. And even further, Jesus gives us this sober warning. If we fail to stand up against world opinion, it will conquer us. We will find ourselves standing in opposition to Jesus himself so that he can't stand with us.

THE
OCTAGON

Jesus invites you to stand with him against world opinion. Will you accept the invitation?

Jesus, this is a challenging invitation. In my heart I know it is right, but it's so hard to do. Sometimes to stand against world opinion involves more than just social consequences. It could even endanger my job and my relationships. Help me to stand in such a way that you are pleased and glorified. Amen.

53

YOUR TOOLBELT

B een into a home improvement store lately? The big
warehouse kind? They're all the rage nowadays, providing almost every tool imaginable, as well as all the things we
use those tools for. Goliath-sized shelves stand packed to the
edge with goods for our home improvement consumption.
Row after row after row, almost anything we could ever need
is right there in one location.

> **Everything that goes into a life of pleasing God has
> been miraculously given to us by getting to know, per-
> sonally and intimately, the One who invited us to God.
> The best invitation we ever received!**
> 2 PETER 1:3 (MSG)

All the product selection in the world is useless if we don't
know how to use what we select. The home improvement
store could have 25 different hammers to choose from, and
we might get the shiniest, nicest, most powerful hammer
they have, complete with rubberized grip, but it won't do us
much good if we're trying to attach a new plate over a light
switch. We also have a need to please God, but if we stick
with trying to use our tools, we're just hammering screws;

our tools aren't going to get the job done. Thankfully, God has invited us into his workshop so we can sit and chat with him for a while. So we can see how exactly he does what he does. So we can get to know him—personally, intimately. The Apostle Peter calls it the best invitation we've ever received. God wants us to please him, but he doesn't want us to do it with our own tools. Instead, he's handed us his toolbox, filled with everything we need, and given us the go-ahead to use everything in there. Peter was right—that is a grand invitation indeed.

ALL
LIFESHAPES

God wants you to use the tools he's given you to please him. Will you do it?

God, you are the Master Builder of my life. I'm so amazed at how you care for me; at how you notice even the littlest things of my life and are already prepared for them. You want me to live a life that pleases you, and I know you wouldn't ask me to do that without giving me the tools to make it happen. Thanks, God. I want to please you, Lord. Amen.

FORGET YOU

Anyone who has flown on an airplane has heard and seen the routine. "In the event of an emergency, the seat cushions can be used as flotation devices. Should we lose cabin pressure, air masks will drop from the overhead compartment. Please put on your own mask first before attempting to help anyone else." You've got to take care of yourself before you can help someone else. What if you passed out while trying to help the person you're sitting next to? You'd both be in trouble! Ironically, this is how most of us live our daily lives.

> "If you don't go all the way with me, through
> thick and thin, you don't deserve me. If your
> first concern is to look after yourself, you'll never
> find yourself. But if you forget about yourself and
> look to me, you'll find both yourself and me."
>
> MATTHEW 10:38-39 (MSG)

Most of us believe it's important to help others. And obviously as Christians we need to be concerned about the people around us. But, when it comes down to it, we generally make sure we're taken care of before concerning ourselves too greatly with others in need. We just don't say it that way. And there is some truth to this thought. But Jesus knows that this rationale is circular. We'll never get fully "fixed" on this planet. Instead, Jesus challenges us to something greater: "If you forget about yourself and look to me, you'll find both yourself and me." What a paradox it is that the road to my healing is to forget about it. How counterintuitive it is that to find myself, I must look away from myself. How amazing it is that I can find who I am by focusing on who someone else is.

THE
TRIANGLE

UP

So Jesus makes this invitation:
"Will you lose yourself and let me find you?"

Jesus, this is an unsafe invitation. You ask me to forget about myself and pay attention to you. You're asking me to lose myself. Yet I'm afraid that I'll stay lost. Help me to trust you. Help me to believe that you're taking care of me so well that I don't have to take care of myself. Amen.

MY FATHER GOD

We all love a rags-to-riches story, especially if it involves children. Take, for example, the famous Broadway musical Annie. Little orphan Annie, the redheaded heroine of the story, lives a hard-knock life in an orphanage under the oppressive thumb of Miss Hannigan. Annie longs for her parents to come back and rescue her from her situation. In the meantime, she takes every opportunity she can to escape from the orphanage, only to be caught and dragged back. Finally, as a gesture of good will, Oliver Warbucks, the richest man in town, agrees to have an orphan stay at his house for Christmas. Guess who that orphan is?

> But whoever did want him, who believed he was who
> he claimed and would do what he said, He made
> to be their true selves, their child-of-God selves.
> These are the God-begotten, not blood-begotten,
> not flesh-begotten, not sex-begotten.
>
> JOHN 1:12-13 (MSG)

The girl with no future was thrust into a lavish life she could never have imagined. And she charmed Warbucks until he adopted her as his own daughter. We're a lot like little Annie, living under the oppression of sin. But God saw our condition and has offered us a life we could never have imagined. He's adopted us and made us his own children. He rescued us from a life we could never have left on our own, no matter how many times we tried, and gave us a life we could only receive through him. He's invited us to become his children. What better Father could we wish for?

THE
HEXAGON

"DADDY"
GOD

The invitation stands. Will you let God adopt you?

God, I know that becoming your child means leaving behind everything in my spiritual orphanage. But I don't care. I know that the life you have for me is so much better. Help me to let go. Help me to let go of my orphanage mentality. Remind me, Lord, that you are my Father, and that you take good care of your children. Thank you, God. Amen.

TAKE A BREAK

A merica is the world's leader in pretty much every category having to do with work and money. We are among the most well-paid, productive, and hard working people on the planet. And we have the homes, cars, and clothes to show for it. America has worked itself into the picture of prosperity. We are an economic "super power." Yet at the same time, over 50 percent of our marriages fail. Addictions and abuses run rampant. Lonely latchkey kids are raised by television and video games. And the threat of violence makes us arm our homes, cars, and offices with sophisticated security systems. And here we are stuck in the middle of it.

"Are you tired? Worn out? Burned out on religion?
Come to me. Get away with me and you'll recover your
life. I'll show you how to take a real rest. Walk with me
and work with me—watch how I do it. Learn the
unforced rhythms of grace. I won't lay anything heavy
or ill-fitting on you. Keep company with me
and you'll learn to live freely and lightly."
MATTHEW 11:28-30 (MSG)

We work hard not only to provide for our families but also to keep our very jobs in a survival-of-the-fittest employment environment. We put in extra hours to gain a little more salary so we can eke out a retirement and somehow put our kids through college at the same time. And during all of this activity we live with the nagging guilt that we need to spend more time with our spouse and kids. It's as if we're on a train, speeding through life so we can get to the next stop to get off and "reset." But a new project always seems to arrive right before the next stop, so we'll have to just survive until the one after. But it never seems to come. Thankfully, Jesus steps in, freezes the flurry of activity racing past us, and invites us: "Come to me. You'll never find rest on your own. Come to me. I'll show you how to rest. I'll show you how to work. I'll give you a rhythm to life so that work and rest are both welcome activities."

Jesus invites you to rest. Will you come?

THE
SEMI-
CIRCLE

REST AND
ABIDE

Jesus, do I ever need this! I need rest. I need a sense of purpose and sanity in the frenetic pace and constant pressures of my life. I'm coming. Show me how to rest. Show me how to work. Show me how to live. Amen.

GOD, I'M THIRSTY

H ave you ever been really thirsty? The kind of thirsty where your body craves refreshment? The dry mouth. The parched throat. The cracked lips. Few feelings in life are as bad or worse than the feeling of thirst. You'd drink hot water straight from a garden hose if it were available. But it has to be water. Soft drinks, juice, milk—none of these things would refresh you. You need water, and you need it fast.

**Jesus said, "Everyone who drinks this water
will get thirsty again and again. Anyone who drinks
the water I give will never thirst—not ever.
The water I give will be an artesian spring within,
gushing fountains of endless life."**
JOHN 4:13-14 (MSG)

When you need water and you finally are able to get some, suddenly things are looking up. You can actually think about something else. There is tangible relief that comes with the quenching of your thirst. Your soul thirsts, too. It craves refreshment as well; fuel to keep it going. Jesus invites you to quench the thirsting of your soul. He holds out the cup to you and says, "Come. Drink. You'll feel so much better." Meanwhile, the world offers many alternatives to Jesus' water, but the soft drinks of sin will never quench your soul's thirst; they will only serve to make it thirstier. Only Jesus offers living water—water that will become a spring within your soul. Not only will your soul receive the refreshment it craves, but it will become healthier and healthier with a constant supply of divine nourishment. You will never thirst again.

THE
HEPTAGON

NUTRITION

Will you accept Jesus' offer of an artesian spring within your soul?

Jesus, I'm tired of living with this constant thirst in my soul. I've tried the sugar-laced drinks of sin, but they aren't getting the job done. I need what you have. I accept what you offer. I want to drink the water that you give. Help me, Jesus. Amen.

LET'S PARTY!

H ave you ever thrown a party and had a poor turnout?
It's not fun. While we may say that we don't really
care, there's something undeniably embarrassing and disap-
pointing about people not showing up. Do they dislike me?
Why wouldn't they want to come? Did I offend somebody?
And to comfort ourselves we construct theories as to why
they didn't show up. Depending on how neurotic and inse-
cure you are or aren't, the list can continue on and on.
These seem to be the usual coping techniques for salving
the wounds of a disappointed host/hostess. But rarely do
you ever hear of someone responding to a poor turnout to
a party by saying, "Let's invite every stranger you run into
and have them come to our party. Drunks, homeless, rude,
inconsiderate, strangers, I don't care. Just ask them to come."

> "God's kingdom," he said, "is like a king who threw a
> wedding banquet for his son. He sent out servants to
> call in all the invited guests. And they wouldn't come!
> . . . Then he told his servants, 'We have a wedding
> banquet all prepared but no guests. The ones I invited
> weren't up to it. Go out into the busiest intersections
> in town and invite anyone you find to the banquet.'

**The servants went out on the streets and rounded up
everyone they laid eyes on, good and bad, regardless.
And so the banquet was on—every place filled."**
MATTHEW 22:2-3, 8-10 (MSG)

Most of us would probably rather just be alone with our
wounded pride than invite strangers into our home just to
be able to say we had a party. But in this parable, we hear
God make a surprising invitation.
We see that God has already invited
people to his kingdom, but has gotten turned down. But God's desire
is for everyone to enter his kingdom.
The unfamiliar, the unworthy, the
unknown—he wants them all to
come. God is quite intent on having
a party, regardless of the company.
And this is great news for us. For we are the lost, the forgotten, the socially awkward, the undesirables. And God wants
us to come.

THE
OCTAGON

God invites you to the party. Will you come?

*God, I'd like to come into your kingdom.
I'm so thankful that you've invited me.
Help me to extend the same invitation
to anyone else you send my way today. Amen.*

LET'S GET MESSY

Serving people seems so lowly, doesn't it? Especially when those people are at a lower station in life than we are. To stoop down and serve them—well, at times it's unthinkable. But we are not an exclusive society. Imagine, for example, a gardener—someone who absolutely adores the taste of fresh vegetables. The gardener would be a fool to look at his garden, snap his fingers, and expect to see vegetables appear. No, the gardener knows he must kneel down and work the soil. He must serve the seed by planting it in the right environment. He must serve the seed by watering it and supplying it with life-giving nourishment. And then, in due time, the seed will serve him by yielding produce.

> "So if I, the Master and Teacher, washed your feet, you must now wash each other's feet. I've laid down a pattern for you. What I've done, you do. I'm only pointing out the obvious. A servant is not ranked above his master; an employee doesn't give orders to the employer. If you understand what I'm telling you, act like it—and live a blessed life."
>
> JOHN 13:14-17 (MSG)

J

If you've
I will soon
ety or dignit
really ever goo
angry, they
long. And if
are embarra
painfully obio
ask the sam
it isn't unco
on end. An
enthusiastic
Jesus was an
of people th
Jesus was th
the Messiah
brought the

One day
he wou
discip
the chi
me. G

It's a messy business for the gardener, one that involves kneeling in the dirt. Soil under the fingernails. Sweat. Toil. But the service is worth it when God increases the seed and causes it to produce for the gardener. Jesus is inviting us to serve. He set the example, and he wants us to follow it. He wants us to stoop down to the dirt, to humble ourselves, to get messy. He did it. We should too. And when we see the benefits of that service, we know we only have God to thank for it. The gardener doesn't make the seed grow—he only gives the seed what it needs, so that it may do what God made it to do. We aren't called to make anyone produce; we're only called to serve. The production is up to the seed. And the One who made it.

THE
SQUARE

Jesus is inviting you to serve. Will you get messy with him?

Lord Jesus, I'm tired of keeping my hands clean. There's just no joy in it. I want to work for you. Help me to humble myself. Help me to stoop down to the places I'm needed. Help me to get my hands messy with all the wonderful seeds — people — that you love so much. I thank you, Jesus, for the opportunity to serve others, just like you did. Amen.

I'M TOO NORMAL

When you were a kid, did you ever dream about being a superhero? Did you imagine yourself using X-ray vision and flying like Superman, or deflecting bullets and running like Wonder Woman? There's something exhilarating about the possibility of doing things that no other human being can do. If we're honest with ourselves, most of us never really outgrow this desire. But instead of fastening a towel around our neck and running through the house, we try to impress our coworkers with our super-human work ethic. Or we demonstrate our otherworldly strength through our involvement in every ministry at the church. We even occasionally let God in on our unique abilities by showing him how often and how long we can pray.

> "When he finally arrives, blazing in beauty and all his
> angels with him, the Son of Man will take his place on
> his glorious throne. . . Then the King will say to those
> on his right, 'Enter, you who are blessed by my Father!
> Take what's come to you in this kingdom. It's been
> ready for you since the world's foundation. And here's
> why: I was hungry and you fed me, I was thirsty and
> you gave me a drink, I was homeless and you gave me a
> room, I was shivering and you gave me clothes, I was
> sick and you stopped to visit, I was in prison and you

came to me.' Then those 'sheep' are going to say,
'Master, what are you talking about? When did we ever
see you hungry and feed you, thirsty and give you a
drink? And when did we ever see you sick or in prison
and come to you?' Then the King will say, 'I'm telling
the solemn truth: Whenever you did one of these things
to someone overlooked or ignored, that was me—
you did it to me.'"

MATTHEW 25:31, 34-40 (MSG)

Despite our best efforts, we usually
end up being more like the comic
sidekick instead of the hero. But in
this passage of scripture, Jesus takes
the pressure off. Jesus lets us know
that the Father isn't looking for super-
heroes. He isn't even looking for the
talented or unique. He's just looking
for someone who can care. These are the true heroes.

THE
PENTAGON

And so Jesus invites you, the normal, to save the world.
Will you?

*Jesus, even though I do believe I have some great
contribution to make to the world, at the same
time I feel like there's nothing I can do. Yet I
hear you saying that the simplest of acts is how
you change the world. Please help me to do
them. Thanks. Amen.*

CAN'T LOVE ENOUGH

Michelle was pregnant—again—and worried. Eight months along, her pregnancy had been fine so far. She was in a happy marriage, and she already had a wonderful little two-year-old girl. No money worries to speak of. Supportive extended family. She had everything she needed to be a great parent to this new child. But she already loved her daughter so, so much. She loved spending time with her little girl. Loved watching her grow up—watching her say her first words, watching her jump up and down in her crib. Michelle couldn't fathom loving any other living thing more than she loved her daughter. What if she didn't have enough love to give to the son she carried in her womb? She felt like she loved the boy already, but was that just because of the pregnancy?

> "This is my command: Love one another the way I loved you. This is the very best way to love. Put your life on the line for your friends. You are my friends when you do the things I command you."
>
> JOHN 15: 12-14 (MSG)

When the imminent day finally arrived and Michelle's son came into this world, she realized her worrying had been in vain. She discovered that the more she loved, the more love she had to give. Instead of depleting her supply of love on her daughter, she'd only grown it to encompass her son. And when she had a third baby two years later, she saw again how much love she had. It's a fact of love that we often forget: we cannot love enough. We always have the capacity to love others, even until our very lives are on the line. Michelle would gladly give up her life for any of her kids; she loves them that much. Jesus gave up his life for all of us. He loved us that much. Let us all love one another, then. Like the family we are.

THE TRIANGLE OUT

Jesus is inviting you to love others. Will you allow him to grow that love within you?

Jesus, I'm so thankful. Thankful and humbled at how much you love me. You put your money where your mouth was, Jesus, and put your life on the line for me. Out of love. Help me to do the same. Jesus, I pray that you'll make this truth about love real for me. Help me to remember that I can't love too much. When it comes to loving others, I can't overdo it. Give me the love I need, Jesus. Amen.

JUST AS I AM

I f you've ever spent any length of time around kids you will soon realize that they have very little sense of propriety or dignity. Kids are as naturally themselves as humans really ever get. If they're hungry, they'll say so. If they're angry, they will yell. If they're happy, they'll laugh loud and long. And if they're sad, tears and wailing will follow. Kids are embarrassingly honest. They ask questions about the painfully obvious, and they don't care how many times they ask the same question. When a child is learning something, it isn't uncommon to hear him repeat it endlessly for hours on end. And kids struggle changing all of this up-front and enthusiastic behavior when someone important is around. Jesus was an important man; he was in demand from throngs of people that clamored for his attention day and night. And Jesus was the heir apparent to the throne of David. He was the Messiah who had come to deliver Israel, and people brought their children to him for his blessing.

> **One day children were brought to Jesus in the hope that
> he would lay hands on them and pray over them. The
> disciples shooed them off. But Jesus intervened: "Let
> the children alone, don't prevent them from coming to
> me. God's kingdom is made up of people like these."**
>
> MATTHEW 19:13-14 (MSG)

If one of us today saw a crowd of kids coming toward the most important man in the world, we might feel the need to quiet them down, too. Yet Jesus shows himself to be someone very different than the disciples might have thought. Instead of thanking the disciples for their hard work in maintaining his professional distance from the "little people," Jesus breaks in and makes a way for the children to get to him. He wanted to be with the silly, loud, short-attention-spanned, smelly-diapered children. What kind of questions do you think they asked Jesus? How still do you think they sat on his lap? Do you think that, miraculously, none of them cried? Probably not; they were just regular kids, and they came to Jesus "as is." And thankfully (or embarrassingly), Jesus invites you to do the same. Because those are the people who are in his kingdom.

THE
CIRCLE

REPENT
AND
BELIEVE

Jesus invites you: Be yourself.

Jesus, I do want to be myself when I'm with you, but something in me resists that. I've learned to say and do the right things as an adult so that I fit in. And I feel like you, especially, expect good behavior. Help me see that you love me just as I am. Thank you. Amen.

ETERNAL GRACE

John and Randy were half brothers. Randy was a product of their mother's first marriage, which failed when he was three. Shortly after, Randy's mother remarried, and soon he had a new little brother, born when he was five and a half years old. As the boys grew, Randy took a liking to his younger sibling, especially because he would always, always, always win at games. They were both competitive, but no matter what the game, Randy always beat John. Being so much younger, John could never muster the strength, skill, or smarts he needed to best his older brother.

> All that passing laws against sin did was produce more lawbreakers. But sin didn't, and doesn't, have a chance in competition with the aggressive forgiveness we call *grace*. When it's sin versus grace, grace wins hands down. All sin can do is threaten us with death, and that's the end of it. Grace, because God is putting everything together again through the Messiah, invites us into life—a life that goes on and on and on, world without end.
>
> ROMANS 5:20-21 (MSG)

Just as Randy would always win sibling competitions hands down, grace always triumphs over sin. Sin doesn't have what it takes to win. Grace is the superior opponent. Grace always wins, hands down. And because of that, God invites us to live a life that never ends. Now eventually, John hit his teens and grew taller than his older brother. Now he was a more even match when the two siblings competed, and sometimes he even won. Likewise, sin can make itself loom larger, make itself appear more competitive. It can even act like

THE
HEXAGON

THE
FATHER'S
KINGDOM

it has won, threatening us with death. But even then, grace is the victor. Because grace opens the door to eternal life. What's the worst that can happen to us? If we die, then we've entered eternal life with God. Thanks to God's invitation, we have it made.

God is inviting you to experience eternal life. Will you take him up on it?

O God, I praise you. I thank you for your blessings. I thank you for defeating sin. I'm so glad that sin is defeated by grace. I'm so glad that my acceptance of your grace gives me eternal life. God, bury this truth deep in my heart. Remind me of it daily, hourly. Thank you for your grace. I look forward to an eternity of getting to know you better. Amen.

SHINE THROUGH ME

Raggle-taggle crowds sit down on a scenic mountainside, listening to a man whose words are different from any they have heard before. In the middle of his sermon, he pauses. Eyes scurry about. He says emphatically, "You are the salt of the earth." Almost all the people turn around to see if he is addressing an invisible group of distinguished rabbinic leaders among them, surely they are not the intended recipients of that honor. He adds, "You are the light of the world." As his gaze burrows into each person on the hillside, they slowly realize that he is talking about . . . them.

> "You are the salt of the earth. But if the salt loses its saltiness, how can it be made salty again? It is no longer good for anything, except to be thrown out and trampled by men. You are the light of the world. A city on a hill cannot be hidden. Neither do people light a lamp and put it under a bowl. Instead they put it on its stand, and it gives light to everyone in the house."
>
> MATTHEW 5:13-15

Many people bow their heads sheepishly as they think of all the things that would disqualify them from such a responsibility: their drunken past, broken relationships, old age. Others are engulfed by their insecurities; they cannot read or write, they are not articulate, they are not as gifted as their neighbor. The remaining few, quite taken aback, can do nothing but begin to ask, "Is this true?" While many continue to muse, the Preacher on the mountainside is still

THE
TRIANGLE

OUT

speaking those same words to the believers that make up this raggle-taggle crowd called "the Church." He sees a broken world as lost as the pilot who remarked, "We're making excellent time; we just don't know where we're going." But he also sees you. He has chosen to live in you. He has chosen to work through you. He has chosen to receive glory through you. What is your response?

His invitation reads, "Shine, I believe in you."

God, it is hard to imagine that you see me, insecurities and all, as one who can bring light to dark places. Help me to embrace this wonderful responsibility and allow you to use me to help those in the world around me. Amen.

CHOOSE TO BELIEVE

C an you think of anything in this world that is eternal? We're so used to seeing beginnings and endings that it's hard to imagine an eternal life. Perpetual. Endless. Timeless. We know these words, but we can't really grasp their definitions, anymore than we can grasp a handful of stars. They are beyond our reach. But perishing . . . that's something we know all about. Every funeral we attend reminds us of our ultimate destiny. Or does it?

> **"For God so loved the world that he gave his one and only Son, that whoever believes in him shall not perish but have eternal life."**
>
> JOHN 3:16

The passage here says that God doesn't want us to perish. Not that he wants to keep us from ever dying physically; he knows we will. He doesn't want us to perish spiritually. He doesn't want us to be separated from him. That's the true definition of perishing. He offers us eternal life. The alternative is eternal death. But either way, whatever we choose, the choice is eternal. That is why he gave us Jesus. His one and only Son, who demonstrated God's love so articulately as to make our eternal choice all the easier. God made us eternal to begin with, and then invited us to come spend that eternity with himself. Think about this: Next Christmas, you'll have to be somewhere. It's unavoidable. Would you rather spend Christmas by yourself, with no food, no shelter, and no presents? Or would you rather spend it with family, in a cozy environment complete with a great dinner and a present or two just for you? We will spend eternity some-where; God is inviting us to spend it with him. Or we can spend it by ourselves. God's choice is clearly the best one.

THE
CIRCLE
BELIEVE

God wants you to spend eternity with him. Would you rather perish instead?

God, thanks for sending Jesus. Thanks for caring enough about me to do that. Thanks for the gift of eternal life. Wow. It's amazing to consider. God, I know I don't get eternity; I can't, really. But whatever it is, I want to spend it with you. And I want others to get there, too. You loved them enough to send Jesus; help me to love them enough to give them information they need to make the right choice. I don't want them to perish, either. Help me to do what I can to keep them from it. Amen.

GOD, LET'S TALK

K ing David wrote, "The LORD is my shepherd, I shall not be in want. He makes me lie down in green pastures, he leads me beside quiet waters, he restores my soul" (Ps. 23:1-3). Is this how you would describe your prayer time? Perhaps like many people, you don't remember what it is like to be alone with God. After pushing the snooze button at least five times this morning, you woke up still exhausted with all kinds of thoughts picking at you. The agonizing hour-long ride to work (which really could be just fifteen minutes if not for the traffic), the reports that were due last week, the bills that must be paid today, the calls that need to be returned, and of course, the children—your children, who you need to pick up from soccer practice this afternoon. These thoughts pick at you all the way to work and when you arrive you realize that you did not take a moment to pray. You throw your hands up; well, you just don't have time and surely God understands.

> "But when you pray, go into your room, close the door
> and pray to your Father, who is unseen. Then your
> Father, who sees what is done in secret, will reward you."
>
> MATTHEW 6:6

Yes, God understands, but your Father longs for time with you. Christ refers to God as "your Father" to remind you that he is interested in having a personal and intimate relationship with you as your Daddy. He does not want you to see your time with him as another chore on the "to do" list, but as a time you get to hang out with your Father, just the two of you; a time to share not only the vexing issues but also the silly joke your six-year-old son told. He would love to do life with you. Will you let him?

THE HEXAGON

His invitation says, "Come, let's talk. What's on your mind?"

Father, thank you for inviting me to spend time with you. My life is so hectic; I feel like I am always running behind. Please help me to seize the opportunities you give me to pray. I would like to know you more intimately. Amen.

I HAVE THE POWER

The United States military is using a brand-new flashlight on some of their heavy machine guns. The new light generates 2,000 lumens, which is about 120 times brighter than your standard flashlight, the kind you buy at the drugstore for two dollars that runs on two D-cell batteries. This new flashlight is a little more than a foot long and weighs roughly three pounds, running on twenty lithium batteries that provide ample power to its xenon gas bulb. And it doesn't even have a filament. It's a marvel of engineering that even makes use of a heat-resistant lens to contain its amazing brightness. This is one amazing flashlight. It's the most powerful flashlight man has ever concocted. Of course, God has a few ideas on power himself:

> He said to them: "It is not for you to know the times
> or dates the Father has set by his own authority. But
> you will receive power when the Holy Spirit comes on
> you; and you will be my witnesses in Jerusalem, and in
> all Judea and Samaria, and to the ends of the earth."
>
> ACTS 1:7-8

God, obviously, knows a thing or two about power—and his power dwarfs anything we can come up with on our own, no matter how good our flashlights get. Jesus said we'll receive power from God—the Holy Spirit—in order to be his witnesses. Jesus wants us to shine brightly, more brightly than anything this world can offer. He'll give us the power to do just that. In fact, when we receive his power, together we can shine God's light to the ends of the earth.

THE PENTAGON

Jesus is inviting you to be a witness. Will you shine for him?

Thanks, Jesus. Thanks for power. Thanks for boldness. Thanks for a purpose in life, part of which is to represent you to this world. I'm ready to do it. I'm ready to shine like the light you've created me to be. I'm appreciative of this chance to shine for you, Jesus. Help me make the most of it as I go through this day. Amen.

TRUST IN ME

I n the midst of life's changes, it is difficult to imagine
worry-free living. When the money is running low and
the bills are due, our sense of responsibility makes us feel
obligated to worry. So we awaken to one miserable sunrise
after another until the pressing issues of the time are
resolved. We take a few breaths and do it all over again,
all the while tacitly persuaded that we ought to look out
for ourselves. Then, on our way home one evening, we
glimpse an eagle in flight and watch the glory of a sunset,
and feel amazed at how much care God took to make them
so beautiful. Yet we resist the thought that he takes even
better care of us!

> **"Therefore I tell you, do not worry about your life,
> what you will eat or drink; or about your body,
> what you will wear. . . . But seek first his kingdom
> and his righteousness, and all these things will be
> given to you as well."**
> MATTHEW 6:25, 33

Christ asks us, "Don't you know you are more valuable to me than a bird or a flower?" Have you ever asked yourself just how much you are worth to God? Do you still question his love for you? Do you think there is a chance that he might not keep his word? He knows of all the experiences that have made us skeptical and he also knows that given the dysfunction in many of our primary relationships we find it difficult to abandon our lives into the hands of someone else. Yet he insists that we trust him. It's as if he is daring us, "Go ahead, abandon yourself to me and see if I will not take care of you." He knows it's scary, but he also knows that complete trust in him and his cause is the only sure way to abundant life.

THE CIRCLE

So God's invitation to you reads, "I know all things. Will you trust me?"

God, I have been let down by people I have trusted in the past and I find it difficult to trust you. I worry about a lot of things that I cannot control instead of just trusting you. I know you love me and I also know that you will never hurt me. Please help me to trust you. Amen.

LET'S REJOICE!

We all have different things that make us happy—perhaps a weekend project in the yard or a slice of watermelon after an hour of swimming. It could be something as simple as driving with the windows down on a lovely spring day or something as complex and multi-leveled as a wedding ceremony. Happiness can be found everywhere. But joy—that's something altogether different now, isn't it? Happiness and joy are merely cousins; we would be mistaken to think they are identical twins. Joy goes deeper, somehow. Happiness is an external thing that happens to us; joy is an internal thing that radiates from us. Joy is a gift of God.

Rejoice in the Lord always. I will say it again: Rejoice!

PHILIPPIANS 4:4

Joy is a condition of the soul, and we must receive it. We are active participants in our soul's joy. We are the valve that controls the amount of joy our souls receive. We must choose it, choose to rejoice in the Lord at all times. In fact, joy is so important that Paul mentions it twice, just to get the point across. He's saying, "You need to rejoice in the Lord, people. Get it? I can't stress this enough: Rejoice!" But what about the act of rejoicing? How do we do it? How do we overcome all the stresses and outside worries of this life to become joyful people? Doesn't that mean we're just ignoring the obvious, hoping it'll go away? Not at all. It means you let God deal with that stuff, like he said he would. Let go; make the decision to rejoice. Always.

THE SEMI-CIRCLE

God's inviting you to experience his joy. Can you let go of your worries and take him up on it?

I need help, God. I need your help to let go of my worries and my cares and my stresses and everything else in my life that threatens to overpower joy. I need your joy, God. I want to obey your Word. I want to rejoice in you at all times. Help me to have your joy. Help me to let go of everything that would keep me from it. Amen.

IT IS HOW IT IS

A re you an honest person? Are you truthful at all times? Face it—even the best of us have told an occasional lie. It is sad that because our society expects us to always "have it together" we are usually at best superficial, and at worst hypocritical. Have you ever found yourself smiling just to feign interest, or laughing at jokes that you know are not funny? Or perhaps, spending time with a group, talking about things you really do not care about, then going home and telling your spouse what a waste of time that was?

> "Again you have heard that is was said to the people
> long ago, 'Do not break your oath, but keep the oaths
> you have made to the Lord.' But I tell you . . . Simply
> let your 'Yes' be 'Yes' and your 'No,' 'No'; anything
> beyond this comes from the evil one."
>
> MATTHEW 5:33-34A, 37

Most of us put on our "best face" on a fairly regular basis. However, in the above passage Christ exposed such "politeness" for what it really is: dishonesty made possible by a compartmentalized life. With the technical expertise of a lawyer, the people had become skilled at separating words or promises made in God's name and those made without it. In fact, people had no problem making a promise they knew full well they did not intend to keep as long as they did not swear by God's name. Christ reminded them that God is in all things. God is involved in all your business, be it at church, at home, at work, in your leisure, and even when you're alone. He is in it all. Because of this, life cannot be categorized and neither can your behavior. Who you are at church, should be who you are at home and who you are at home should be who you are at work, and who you are at work should be who you are in your leisure. Although your roles may be different, would you say you are the same person in all places?

THE
CIRCLE

Christ invites you to "keep it real."

God, I never really thought of some of the things that I do as dishonest, but now I see it. You really are in all things! Please teach me how to love truth and to live an honest life. Amen.

YOU DEAL WITH IT

Stress is fashionable. Bookstores feature entire sections filled with books on stress relief. Late night television is rife with infomercials advertising some method of eliminating it. Medications, tape series, Internet websites, neighborly advice . . . seems like everyone is selling contentment. And it also seems like everyone else is buying it—again and again. The first one doesn't work, so they try another one. And then another one. And then another one. But the stresses continue to build upon each other, negating each new quick fix.

> **Do not be anxious about anything, but in everything,**
> **by prayer and petition, with thanksgiving,**
> **present your requests to God.**
>
> PHILIPPIANS 4:6

Our culture is set upon stress. Even Christians are, though we're supposed to turn down stress whenever it tries to put the moves on us. God has invited us to live a contented life, a rested, relaxed life that negates the powers of stress. And he's plain about how to get there, too: it all hinges on prayer. Stressed about something? Pray about it. Take it before the

Lord's throne. Ask the King of all glory to take care of it for you. There's nothing he can't do. You have the opportunity to live a completely contented life; it's just a matter of approaching it the correct way. Sure, some of those stress-relief books have some valid things to say. Yes, there is some truth in what the infomercials say. Even the medications have their correct applications. But God's ultimate prescription is simply a conversation with him.

THE HEXAGON

THE FATHER'S KINGDOM

God wants you to be passionately content with your life. Do you?

I like the sound of contentment, God. I'm so thankful that you care about my life like that. You want me to be rid of the anxieties that weigh me down. I take those stresses to you right now. Lord, I confess those to you. I give them to you. Please take them from me. I don't want them anymore. Thank you for replacing them with contentment. True contentment that only you can give. Amen.

LIVE IN ME

After getting glued to her seat by her unruly high school music class, the humiliated Sister Mary Clarence in the movie *Sister Act 2*, on being consoled by her fellow nuns, remarked that the only thing she hated was that there was nothing to pick up and throw. Have you ever found yourself voraciously looking for something to throw back at the people who've hurt you? Or perhaps you would rather take the more "dignified" route of simply walking around with a chip on both shoulders?

> **"If you love those who love you, what reward will you get? Are not even the tax collectors doing that? And if you greet only your brothers, what are you doing more than others? Do not even pagans do that? Be perfect, therefore, as your heavenly Father is perfect."**
>
> MATTHEW 5: 46-48

Every Christian has been told that the distinguishing mark of a believer is the presence of love in their life. There is no doubt that this teaching rings in your ears when you have encounters with the rude store clerk, or the smart-alecky coworker. Needless to say, not having a comeback to "put them in their place" takes a swing at your pride and brings your blood to a boil. Then the gentle whisper of the Holy Spirit reminds you of how God, in his infinite mercy, chooses to let his sun shine on both the rude store clerk and the kind old man alike. And you hear the words, "Now you go and do likewise." A strange feeling of discomfort overwhelms you because you recognize that doing likewise will make you look weak. Yet if you looked beyond the shifting shadows of weakness you would find yourself gazing into the dawn of true spiritual maturity. God wants you to become like him and discover the higher and perfect path of love and forgiveness for all people at all times. Do you want to be like him?

THE
HEXAGON

THE
FATHER'S
FORGIVENESS

His invitation says, "I am Love. Come live in me."

God, I know that you are a God of love and forgiveness and I have to admit that loving people can be really hard. Teach me to be a more loving person, to love all people no matter how good or bad they are. Thanks for loving and forgiving me even when I can't do the same for myself. Amen.

LET IT GO

Travis's arms ached. His fingers felt swollen. His feet, abused. His heart, exhilarated. He'd never been to Spain, and now he was walking the streets of Barcelona, having arrived to spend two weeks in evangelistic ministry at the 1992 Summer Olympic Games. But first things first—he was meeting some missionaries from Madrid to deliver two full suitcases of luxuries from home. A family member had asked him to be the go-between, taking clothes, baked goods, cards, letters, and other special things to the missionaries, and he'd agreed. But the walk was starting to take its toll. The suitcases were heavy to begin with and, a mile into this uphill climb from the train station, felt like they might slip out of his hands. Finally, Travis's group reached the ministry site. The missionaries greeted him and took over the load. The instant the suitcases left his hands, he felt such relief. Could he fly? It felt like it. The lifting of the weight was one of the most blessed feelings he'd ever felt.

**And the peace of God, which transcends all
understanding, will guard your hearts
and your minds in Christ Jesus.**

PHILIPPIANS 4:7

As we journey through this life, sin, stress, and outside pressures threaten to weigh us down, slow our progress, get us to stop. But God directs us to let him take the weight. Jesus walks along with us, offering to grab those suitcases. We don't need to carry them; he wants them. We just have to give them to him through prayer. And then we can journey on in peace. A peace that surpasses our knowledge. Travis had never known the feeling he felt when he finally gave up those suitcases, because he'd never lifted so much weight for so long before. And the knowledge that he was free of the burden gave him a peace about it that helped ready him for the rest of his trip. When we give our weights to God, they become his responsibility, not ours. We are through with them. We can live a peaceful, passionate life.

THE
HEPTAGON

EXCRETION

Jesus is inviting you to give him your baggage. Will you let him take it?

Jesus, here I am. I'm standing here with falsely claimed luggage. This doesn't belong to me; I picked it up off the carousel without thinking. I can see that this is supposed to be yours, so I'm giving it back to you. Please take it from me. Give me peace. Give me the peace that comes with losing my burden. I praise you for it, Jesus. I love you. Amen.

ONE DAY AT A TIME

O ne of the greatest tragedies of the human experience is that it often takes calamity to remind us that we ought to treasure each day of our lives. When we hear of the death of a young mother we lament, "Life is so short." Yet, in the absence of tragedy, we go back to living on autopilot, regretting yesterday or worrying about tomorrow. In the meantime, the present passes us by. The days turn into weeks and the weeks into months, and then one soft spring day, as we breathe in the untainted air, we take a look back at the road most traveled and sigh. The mortgage was paid. The dog did not die. The kids were not crushed. We did not go hungry. What if it really is true that 95 percent of the things people worry about never happen? What a waste of mental energy!

> **"Therefore do not worry about tomorrow,
> for tomorrow will worry about itself. Each
> day has enough trouble of its own."**
> MATTHEW 6:34

Do you ever ask yourself, "Why do I worry?" Could it be because your security is threatened and you're afraid? Christ knew that fear lay at the heart of worry and lovingly took the pressure off us by reminding us that we have neither the power to control the future, nor the ability to add a single hour to our life! Christ wants you to settle the nagging question of who is in control of your future. Do you believe that your future is secure in Christ? If so, take a look around, enjoy the sprouting spring flowers, frame your two-year-old's masterpiece and go ahead and have some cheesecake! Live one day at a time, resting secure in the arms of the One who holds the future.

THE
CIRCLE

God invites you to enjoy the present.

God, thank you for the gift of life. What a marvelous gift! Forgive me for living as though my future is in my hands. There are so many things that I am afraid of. Please help me to put my mind at rest and enjoy each day. Amen.

97

CAN I HAVE SOME GUM?

H ave you ever asked children to share their candy with you? They could be unwrapping some gum or munching on a chocolate bar or opening a package of jelly-beans, and the second you ask them if you can have some, they instinctively clutch it to their chest. After all, it's theirs, not yours. If you wanted some, you should have gotten your own. But then again, Mommy and Daddy always say that it's good to share. "Okay, you can have some, but just a little bit," they finally say. And then they'll give you one jellybean, or a small corner of the chocolate bar, or a micron of gum. Yes, a good deed done.

> **Yet it was good of you to share in my troubles.**
> **Moreover, as you Philippians know, in the early days**
> **of your acquaintance with the gospel, when I set out**
> **from Macedonia, not one church shared with me in**
> **the matter of giving and receiving, except you only;**
> **for even when I was in Thessalonica, you sent me**
> **aid again and again when I was in need.**
> PHILIPPIANS 4:14-16

The funny thing about sharing is that we don't really get better as adults. We might be freer with our candy, but there are other things we're less free with. Time is often a casualty. Hard to share that. Love? Impossible, almost. Money? Well, don't call it sharing; call it a loan—with interest—and you have a deal. Small things are nothing; we'll share those all day long. But the important things, the things God wants us to share, those are tougher calls. He wants us to be passionate about proving our love for one another by sharing what we have with each other. There's an old story about a group of people that didn't have much to eat. One family had some meat. Another only had a bunch of carrots. Another family had a few potatoes. Individually, these families didn't have much. Together, they had a stew. This is the type of attitude God is inviting us into: an attitude of sharing. An attitude that acknowledges that everything we have belongs to God, not us. That we should use it as he sees fit, not as we do. This is the crux of generosity.

THE
TRIANGLE

OUT

An invitation to be generous stands before you. Will you accept it?

Jesus, I do accept your offer to be generous. Thank you for all the blessings you've given me. Thank you for giving me everything I have. I recognize that it's all on loan from you, and that if you want me to pass it on to someone else, I'll do that. I just want to follow your will, Lord. Thank you. Amen.

JUST ASK

A four-year-old boy approaches his dad and says, "Dad if it's not too much trouble, I was wondering if you could help me tie my shoelaces; I really hate to bother you, but would that be OK?" If we heard this, most of us would be perturbed. We would not only wonder why this child is afraid of his dad but we would also chastise his dad for the bad example that he is! Ironically, many of us approach God the same way. We bow our heads timidly and bite the nail on our pinky finger as we make our request.

> **"Ask and it will be given to you; seek and you will find;**
> **knock and the door will be opened to you."**
>
> MATTHEW 7:7

Sometimes, when the darkness in our lives seems total, our prayers begin to sound more like wild incantations uttered to a tight-fisted god whose fingers must be pried open. Because we become inaccessible to reason during these times, we forget that we are speaking to a Father who not only loves us but has also given us the right to approach him boldly. Do you know that you have the attention of the King of the Universe whenever you want it? You could be beneath the thundering waters of Niagara Falls, bungee jumping from New Zealand's mountain peaks, or smack-dab in the middle of a crisis you put yourself in and his attention is yours for the asking. Isn't that incredible? Christ admonishes us to be persistent; keep on asking, keep on seeking, keep on knocking. How much have you given up on in prayer because you've assumed that God will not give it to you? Today, he looks at you and says, "Need something? Ask me." Yes, he does love you that much.

THE
HEXAGON

THE
FATHER'S
PROVISION

God's invitation is simple: "What can I do for you?"

Thank you, Father, for your kindness. I am glad that I don't have to feel like I am bothering you each time I bring a need to you. Help me never to forget that you are more willing to give than I am to ask. Amen.

US AGAINST THEM

We've all heard about how Christians are to "go against the flow." Like salmon. When the time comes for salmon to spawn and reproduce, they swim from the ocean to their homes—upstream all the way. It is a journey of thousands of miles. Along the way, the salmon must evade predators. The salmon don't even eat, so focused are they on the mission that is ingrained in them. Each inch they move is a battle, a fight against river currents and sharp-eyed bears. But the salmon don't stop until they finally reach their goal: the breeding grounds. There, the fight has been worth it. They're bruised. Battered. Exhausted. But they've achieved their goal.

> **Do not conform any longer to the pattern of this world,**
> **but be transformed by the renewing of your mind.**
> **Then you will be able to test and approve what God's**
> **will is—his good, pleasing and perfect will.**
>
> ROMANS 12:2

God has invited us into a revolution like this. He's called us to think differently from the world, to set ourselves apart, to fight the current of conformity the world would have us flow in. As we focus on God's Word and the life-changing effects it offers us, we are giving ourselves fuel for the battle. We are called to swim in a counter-current direction, for that is the direction our treasure lies. When salmon finally reach their breeding grounds, they dig a hole to lay their eggs. That final act is what kills them. There they lie, dead and rotting. But that is just the thing their eggs need to hatch. New life is brought about from that death. And it's the same for us. We're called to fight against the world's current each day. We're called to die to ourselves each day. And from that death comes new life; a life that couldn't exist without the death that preceded it. This is God's way. This is God's will. This is God's passion. This is God's invitation.

THE HEPTAGON

God's inviting you to swim against the current of the world. Will you fight the current?

God, this sounds pretty tough. Looking at the world around me, I sometimes feel like jumping in. Like sin is inevitable. Help me to put aside that mindset. As I dig into your Word, Lord, help me to focus on fighting the current of this world. Give me the focus I need to make it home. Thank you, Lord, for your blessings. Thank you for the strength I need. Amen.

SHOW ME HOW

Have you ever thought about how you would like to be treated? Would you like people to forgive you for some of the foolish things you've said or done? Do you want them to realize that that it's not really what you believe? Would you like them to listen to you and consider the things you say, not just pretend? Would you like them to be a little gentler with you? Would you like them to allow you to just be yourself? If your answer is "yes," then consider this: is this how you treat them?

> **"So in everything, do to others what you**
> **would have them do to you, for this sums**
> **up the Law and the Prophets."**
> MATTHEW 7:12

This verse is probably one of the most quoted passages of the Bible. Unfortunately, it is often used during those times when someone gets back negative consequences for negative actions. "See," we taunt, "do unto others . . ." And we completely miss the point. Most of us don't treat people well most of the time. And most of the time, we focus on the things that we do not do. We do not yell at them. We are not rude to them. Although we may not be listening, we are polite enough to keep quiet while they talk. Christ however, challenges us to the higher path of doing. Instead of simply not being rude to your spouse, you could buy them a gift to remind them of how much you appreciate them. Instead of politely being quiet as they speak, you could actually listen to what they are saying. There is no doubt that this kind of behavior cannot be manufactured; it is the kind that can only come from a life that is immersed in the love of God. Ask God to teach you how to love.

THE HEPTAGON

SENSITIVITY

God's invitation says, "There is a better way. Follow me and I'll show you."

God, loving and treating people right takes a lot of effort and discipline. Help me to learn from you; I know I could never do it on my own. Amen.

IT'S GOOD FOR YOU

T here are five *Rocky* movies. Five. Toward the end, each of them tells pretty much the same story. And so does every other sports movie, or kung-fu movie, or action movie. The hero of our story has been through the wringer, and now they're facing off with the big guy—their mortal enemy. The one person they've been hoping to get a shot at. The fight begins, and our hero gets a few early shots in. This is looking good for him! But then—oh, no! He's taking a few blows! There's blood on his lip! He's getting the stuffing beat out of him! It's almost over; the bad guy's going to win! But wait. Wait! Our hero—he's . . . he's making a comeback! He's fighting through the pain and pummeling the bad guy now. And the bad guy's really shocked. He can't believe what's going on. Our hero is fighting with all he has now! It's looks like . . . Yes! He won!

> **We are hard pressed on every side, but not crushed; perplexed, but not in despair; persecuted, but not abandoned; struck down, but not destroyed. We always carry around in our body the death of Jesus, so that the life of Jesus may also be revealed in our body.**
>
> 2 CORINTHIANS 4:8-10

No matter how many times we see it, we always cheer when our hero wins the victory. He was pressed hard on every side, but he wasn't crushed. He was perplexed, but he wasn't in despair. He got knocked down, to be sure, but he wasn't destroyed. Jesus is inviting us into this situation. We can have victory, too! But not in a shallow, movie-like way. Jesus is inviting us to suffer along with him, to get the stuffing beat out of us once in a while. Because it will happen. But when it does, we can rest in knowing that we have the ultimate victory. Suffering can and will cause pain, but Jesus has won the contest, and we know that suffering is only temporary. His victory is eternal.

THE SQUARE

Jesus is inviting you to suffer with him. Are you willing to do it?

Scary, Lord. This is a scary idea. I'm not sure I like the sound of this. Suffering—it sounds so real and painful. Nevertheless, you endured more suffering than I ever could. Help me to focus on what's really going on when I suffer for your name's sake. Even if it's just a few taunts about you or whatever, help me to represent you well. And help me to remember the ultimate prize: heaven. Amen.

DON'T STOP NOW

How many of us have listened to a great sermon and, swept by the emotional tide, made a commitment to do what the preacher said? Then on Monday morning, when the stark realities of life bite us in the armpit and the emotion subsides, we are no longer sure if we even believe what the preacher said! The marketing industry knows something about our impetuousness and plays well upon it. They get us excited about their products with promises of fabulous bodies, softer and firmer skin, and a sure path to success. After we make the purchase, we realize that far from being a good deal, what we have is an hour-long disappointment. We make plans to send it back.

> When Jesus saw the crowd around him, he gave orders
> to cross to the other side of the lake. Then a teacher of
> the law came to him and said, "Teacher, I will follow
> you wherever you go." . . . But Jesus told him,
> "Follow me, and let the dead bury their own dead."
>
> MATTHEW 8:18-19, 22

Like many of the others in the crowd, this teacher was fascinated by the words of Christ; he wanted to go wherever Christ was going. Christ, however, being familiar with our fickleness, when confronted by a volunteer, made sure to give him raw details of what discipleship wasn't. It was not going to be a perpetual state of bliss. In fact, it would be a life of persecution and constantly choosing to do the right thing when it would be easier to do wrong. Quite a campaign slogan! Christ wanted committed followers who would be in it for the long haul, not those who would abandon ship at the first test of honor. Are you in it for the long haul? Is God moving upon your heart to give up something today? Do it! Keep following and let him take you on the most exhilarating journey of your life.

THE
CIRCLE

KAIROS

God's invitation to you says, "If you want to go on the greatest adventure of your life, follow me!"

Father, being a disciple can be really tough. Please keep me steady and help me to remember that the joys and rewards of following you far outweigh the sorrows. Amen.

YOU'RE WORTH IT

M any people will agree that great leaders are often great visionaries—people with the ability to see what others cannot see. When people saw Matthew, they saw everything disgraceful about the current system; they saw a corrupt extortionist and a vulture that fed on the flesh of his own people. Yet, when Christ saw him, he saw a disciple—someone worth calling to be a fisher of men— and he approached Matthew as though he already were these things. Jesus did not hang his sins over his head to bring him to repentance; he simply had lunch with him.

As Jesus went on from there, he saw a man named Matthew sitting at the tax collector's booth. "Follow me," he told him, and Matthew got up and followed him. While Jesus was having dinner at Matthew's house, many tax collectors and "sinners" came and ate with him and his disciples. When the Pharisees saw this, they asked his disciples, "Why does your teacher eat with tax collectors and 'sinners'?" On hearing this, Jesus said, "It is not the healthy who need a doctor, but the sick. But go and learn what this means: 'I desire mercy, not sacrifice.' For I have not come to call the righteous, but sinners."

MATTHEW 9:9-13

Many times it is difficult to see our lives for all they are worth, considering that we have enough failures and missteps over our shoulders to confirm that we can only be so much. God however, sees past all our weaknesses and sees the great potential that we have and what we could be if we were put on the right track. Take a moment to examine where you are today. Reflect on the choices you have made that have brought you to this point. Do you, like Matthew, need to start moving in a direction different from the one that you've been going in? While the cynics of the day debated on the ethics of Christ's involvement with Matthew, the Master Visionary was reeling into the kingdom of God a man who would later tell his story. Instead of wallowing in the guilt of your past, will you believe what God says about you? Despite popular opinion that you should be lost, God loves you enough to still come after you.

THE CIRCLE

God's invitation to you says, "I have a place with your name on it. Come see it."

God, thank you so much for not holding my past mistakes against me. Please help me to believe that I can be more than what I am right now, and that you have a place for me where my talents can best be used for your glory. Amen.

REVEALED IN YOU

Have you ever been to the Grand Canyon? It's a breath-taking sight—one of the seven natural wonders of the world. We might look at it and think of the strength it represents; it is indeed a massive gorge, about 277 miles long, ranging between four and eighteen miles wide and almost a mile deep. Despite this amazing, gigantic wonder, the Grand Canyon is a picture of weakness. That rock could not stand up to the meager Colorado River, which has worn it down over the years until it became what it is today: a big object lesson in hardship.

> But he said to me, "My grace is sufficient for you,
> for my power is made perfect in weakness." Therefore
> I will boast all the more gladly about my weaknesses,
> so that Christ's power may rest on me. That is why,
> for Christ's sake, I delight in weaknesses, in insults,
> in hardships, in persecutions, in difficulties.
> For when I am weak, then I am strong.
>
> 2 CORINTHIANS 12:9-10

The world will try to persecute us, insult us, bring us hardships, wear us down. But the more the world tries to do that, the more it carves us into something more beautiful than we would ever have been. Without the hardships, without the difficulties, we would be flat land. We would be boring desert. But now, with the persecution, with the insults, our weaknesses are made into strengths. God's strength, operating through our weaknesses, will cause people to take note of us. The more our weaknesses are exposed, the greater God's strength grows, in order to balance them out. And therefore, the weaker we are, the greater God is. We cannot do this on our own, and if we try, we only deceive ourselves. Let us be grand canyons; let us glory in our weaknesses, that Christ's power may rest on us.

THE
CIRCLE

God's inviting you to be weak for his sake. Are you strong enough to take the challenge?

Dear Jesus, I thank you for sending your power to rest on me. I acknowledge that I'm weak. I can't do life on my own. I need your strength. In fact, the more of your strength I get, the better. So help me to be weak for your sake. Help me to delight in my weaknesses and not cover them up. Help me to be an authentic person, on display for your glory. I love you, Lord, and I give you all the praise. Amen.

113

BECOME BROKEN

C hrist knows the human heart all too well. He knows about the self-satisfied piety that is seen when people look upon others and evaluate them based on self-promoting criteria. Educational background, knowledge of Scripture, or even marital status is the instrument by which they determine how much higher up the spiritual ladder they are. They smile contentedly, happy that they are "better" than one more person and certain that they have nothing in common with the "less spiritual." Have you ever caught yourself thinking this way? Interestingly, God, who is infinitely perfect in every way and whose excellent beauty is unequalled, chooses to be associated with the less spiritual.

> **"But go and learn what this means: 'I desire mercy,
> not sacrifice.' For I have not come to call the righteous
> but sinners."**
> MATTHEW 9:13

God wants to be with those who recognize that they do not have it together, those who have missed their devotions more times than they wish to count, those who were only able to fast one meal instead of forty days, those who have sinned enough times to realize that they have nothing to prove, those whose eyes are simply looking to him for help. When you encounter these people, what do you see? The self-satisfied see people needing pity. God sees grateful recipients of his mercy. God is not impressed by our religious performances. He does care about how we treat the despised people among us; the uneducated factory worker at the bottom of the socioeconomic ladder, the shamefaced teenage mother, the ex-con who's living under a bridge because no one will employ him. When you see them, do you take pride in your place in the universe or does his mercy overwhelm you? Mercy is drawn to brokenness.

God invites you to be merciful just as he is merciful.

THE
HEPTAGON

GROWTH

God, please forgive me for the times when I have despised people and taken pride in things that do not matter. Please help me to see people the way you see them. Thank you for being merciful to me. Amen.

FREE FROM SIN

In the hit movie *Secondhand Lions*, two retired and ornery brothers, who had returned from a forty-year stint in Africa, order a used lion so they can relive their days of safari adventure. In a moment of intense drama, their great-nephew, Walter, throws open the lion's crate to release the big cat. But the lion doesn't run for it. She just stays in that crate. Instead of presenting a challenging snarl, all she comes up with is a juicy belch. The would-be hunters stare at her, completely befuddled. It's like the creature has forgotten what she is and what she was made to be. From that moment on, the brothers' great-nephew, Walter, looks after the lion whom he named Jasmine.

**It is for freedom that Christ has set us free.
Stand firm, then, and do not let yourselves
be burdened again by a yoke of slavery.**

GALATIANS 5:1

Jasmine seems to think she has it pretty good there in that dark little crate. But it's not until she leaves the wooden cage that she finally becomes what she was made to be: a "real Africa lion." And her last moment becomes her greatest; she dies saving Walter's life.

THE
HEXAGON

THE
FATHER'S
FORGIVENESS

How often do we willingly stay in the crates of sin that we've been freed from? Jesus set us free, and we should resist the chains and slavery of sin with all that is in us. We should resist with the strength that Christ gives us. Let us stand firm and stay unburdened.

Lord God, I want to remain free from sin. Those chains, that prison—they have nothing for me. God, help me to stand firm on your ground. I thank you for purchasing my freedom, simply for freedom's sake. I love this freedom, God. I want to live in it forever. Thank you. Amen.

117

CELEBRATE LIFE

J im could hear the music from a block away; the air was so alive he could hear it sing. As he approached, he saw people everywhere; the women in their finest and the men not easily outdone. Ribbons and flowers overwhelmed an elaborate cake display. And the food! Jim could sniff out a peppered steak faster than any hound ever could. As his mouth began to water, Jim spotted the happy couple and he knew he had arrived at a party. Like Jim, everyone loves a wedding celebration; we love the sense of joy and celebration draw us to them. Interestingly, Christ likens our time with him to a wedding.

> **Jesus answered, "How can the guests of the
> bridegroom mourn while he is with them?
> The time will come when the bridegroom will
> be taken from them; then they will fast."**
>
> MATTHEW 9:15

Can you imagine what a party with Christ is like? This is probably hard for many to grasp because they see too many examples of believers whose lives are not only dull, but who also look like they are constantly in crisis. Christ desires that you celebrate life. Do you walk with a bounce in your step and a smile on your face? Do you realize that you have a lot to celebrate? Because of Christ, you have hope for a bright future. Because of Christ, you can be sure that your problems are only temporary. Because of Christ, you have a reason for living. All these reasons and more are a cause for celebration. The day will soon come when we will be in heaven's ballroom, mesmerized by the sparkle of diamonds and sapphire, staring at mountain peaks at once golden and frosted, feasting on heaven's finest mignon, listening to the angelic host sing to the King. But for now, the party still goes on.

THE
HEXAGON

THE
FATHER'S
CHARACTER

Christ says, "Let's celebrate!"

God, thank you for all the joy you bring to my life. When things are going wrong in my life, please help me to remember that because I have you, I can still celebrate life. Amen.

KNOW FULLNESS

H ave you ever rented a "Jupiter Jump" for a child's birthday party or other event? A big, square, inflatable trampoline with inflatable walls. It rests on the ground, and the kids climb into it and hop around. It's great fun and usually is the hit of any birthday party. And they're fascinating to watch as they're being blown up. Because of their size, they require a special fan that blows continuous air into them. They come rolled up into a surprisingly small cylinder. Then they're unrolled, and the fan is hooked up and turned on. Slowly, almost majestically, they begin to rise from their flat position on the ground and take shape. They lean this way and that while the air fills them, but soon they're fully inflated and ready for business.

> I ask him to strengthen you by his Spirit—not a brute strength but a glorious inner strength—that Christ will live in you as you open the door and invite him in. And I ask him that with both feet planted firmly on love, you'll be able to take in with all Christians the extravagant dimensions of Christ's love. Reach out and experience the breadth! Test its length! Plumb the depths! Rise to the heights! Live full lives, full in the fullness of God.
>
> EPHESIANS 3:16-19 (MSG)

From one fan, that entire trampoline had been completely inflated, from corner to corner and everywhere in between. Nothing was left behind; no quadrant remained unchanged by the force of the air rushing into it. God would will that our lives be the same way—that we would experience the same fullness of life from him. That we would know the extravagant dimensions of Christ's love, that we would allow it to rush through every part of us, and in so doing, that we would take our true shapes. We started this life flat and lifeless; Christ gives us what we need to do what we were designed to do. It starts with fullness.

THE
CIRCLE

God is inviting you to experience his fullness. Will you let him in?

Jesus, I'm tired of living a flat, off-balance life. I want to be full. I want you to invade every part of my soul. Leave nothing deflated, Lord. Make me into the true, full shape you've designed me to have. I'm so thankful, and I praise you. Amen.

GOT ANY CHANGE?

When driving to work each morning, do you use the same route? Do you sit in the same seat when you go to church? Do you order the same meal each time you visit a restaurant? Are you going to the same Colorado cabin that you've been to ten times in the last ten years for this year's vacation? If you answered, "Yes" to these questions, you are probably the kind that walks around with an enigmatic expression whenever a major change happens!

> **"No one sews a patch of unshrunk cloth on an old garment, for the patch will pull away from the garment, making the tear worse."**
> MATTHEW 9:16

We tend to find security in things that have been there for a long time. Even when they prove to be lacking, we would rather stick with them. Christ however, breaks into this pattern of thinking and opens our eyes to a new paradigm: you can only patch a garment for so long. There comes a time when the garment must be thrown away because patching it will do more harm than good. For example, instead of changing churches, perhaps what needs to change is your perspective of what church is truly about; perhaps your relationship with Jesus needs to be redefined from "religious activity" to the common thread that binds the tapestry of your life together; perhaps you need to change your attitude and actions toward your wife or husband. In the absence of such change, we cease to grow. Are there areas of your life that need an "extreme makeover?"

THE
HEPTAGON

MOVEMENT

God's invitation says, "I'm doing a new thing! Come and be a part."

God, help me to open my mind and embrace the changes that you want to bring into my life. Amen.

WALK WITH ME

It's tough to have a conversation without light, isn't it? Words lose the added dimensions of body language and facial expressions. We've all had times where we've had a midnight chat with a friend, or with a spouse before bed. While those times are fine in their own right, they aren't really the ideal way to communicate all the time. It's very difficult to truly fellowship with others under those conditions.

> **But if we walk in the light, as he is in the light, we have fellowship with one another, and the blood of Jesus, his Son, purifies us from all sin.**
>
> 1 JOHN 1:7

We all have dark places in our lives we'd rather keep to ourselves. Jesus is inviting us to come into the light, into the places where true fellowship takes place. He's inviting us to let him shine his light into all our dark places. He's inviting us to live a life of light, so that we might showcase his strength and his triumph over sin. We're not kidding anyone when we pretend that we're sinless. Everyone has some sin in their lives, so let's just deal with it—here in the light of

Christ—so we can move on. As we fellowship with each other we begin to build an honest and authentic community where accountability and transparency thrive. God created us to live life together, not stuck isolated in boxes and compartments where certain people only get to "see" certain things. As we walk honestly "in the light" about our sins and the things of our lives that we want to change, we experience the true nature of fellowship. This is what we're called to do.

THE
CIRCLE

Jesus invites you to walk in the light with him. Will you give him your darkness?

Lord, it's so hard. There are things I have, dark places within me, that I don't know if I can trust with others. I really want to walk in the light with you, though. I want to be rid of my sin. I expose that to your light right now, Lord. Thank you for accepting it. Thank you for purifying me and my brothers and sisters in you. Thank, Jesus, for all you've done for us. Thank you for your light. Amen.

HARVEST TIME

Scottish theologian William Barclay told the story of the friend of the great reformer Martin Luther, who made a passionate commitment that while Luther was out bleeding and working his hands rough in the battle for the reformation of the church, he would remain in the safety of the monastery praying for him. Both monks held up their part of the deal, until one night when Luther's friend had a dream. He dreamt of an extensive cornfield, the size of the world, and in it was one man trying to reap the harvest. The efforts of this man were admirable, but he could tell the task was impossible. When he saw the face of the reaper, it was the face of Martin Luther. This dream left such an impression on the young monk that not too long afterwards he left the monastery and joined the lone reaper in the field.

> **When he saw the crowds, he had compassion on them,**
> **because they were harassed and helpless, like sheep**
> **without a shepherd. Then he said to his disciples,**
> **"The harvest is plentiful but the workers are few.**
> **Ask the Lord of the harvest therefore, to send out**
> **workers into his harvest field."**
> MATTHEW 9:36-38

Like the young monk, would you rather pray behind closed doors away from the action and give someone the money to do the reaping? Sure, prayer and financial support are important. Christ, in his deep compassion for the helpless sheep, wants us to understand that reaping is a team effort; even the best of players could not win the game alone. Many are unable to cross the seas because of family commitments and work-related responsibilities but there is a lot more to reaping than crossing seas, most of the time crossing the street to visit the widow in her distress or leaning over a desk to invite a coworker to worship is worth a day in the field. All Christ is looking for are willing laborers.

THE
OCTAGON

God's invitation to you says, "Come and join in, it's harvest time."

God, forgive me for not doing my part in reaping the harvest. Open my eyes so that I may see the harvest opportunities you place in my path. Amen.

LEAD WITH COURAGE

L et us imagine for a moment that you are the owner of a very successful restaurant. You've gotten good reviews. You have a steady stream of regular clientele and newcomers who become regulars. You've perfected your menu down to the last side item, and every server you've hired has worked out splendidly. And then someone comes in off the street and tells you that you're doing everything wrong. You should be selling carpet, targeting all the general contractors in your area. Also, you have the wrong salespeople. And you should probably get a forklift or two. Obviously you'd let this person know that their suggested changes are ridiculous and, after determining whether they were joking or not, show them the door.

**If anyone shows up who doesn't hold to this teaching,
don't invite him in and give him the run of the place.**
2 JOHN 1:10 (MSG)

Jesus is inviting you into a leadership role regarding the teachings of his Word. He's made you the owner of your particular restaurant, and he's put you in charge of keeping things on track. If someone comes to you giving you teachings that stray from the Bible, you've been charged to stand firm. Show some leadership. Resist those teachings. Show them the door, because you're in charge and your restaurant isn't changing. You're willing to add new things to the menu as you learn about them, you're willing to upgrade the table settings when they need it, but you will not change the nature of your establishment—about that there

THE
SQUARE

can be no debate. Jesus wants you to be passionate about your faith and about the way you treat the wayward teachings of some. He wants you to be loving but firm. Jesus wants you to hold fast to the things you know. They are precious to you—and to him.

Will you passionately defend what you hold dear?

Jesus, I know there will be times in my life when the devil will try to sway me. He may be subtle, or he may be bold. Either way, I pray that you'll give me the wisdom and discernment to know when he tries. And help me to hold true to this promise: that I will always hold on to you, Jesus. No matter what. I will hold on. I love you too much to let go. Amen.

OUR CROSS TO BEAR

Have you ever wondered what it must be like being a Christian in a time and place where you could be killed for it? Church history has recorded numerous gruesome tales about martyrs who were tortured and killed for their faith. Although, by God's mercy, most of us will never see such a day, none of us are exempt from carrying our cross. With the seriousness of a judge and the conviction of a prophet, Christ uncompromisingly lays down discipleship's ultimate requirement: the carrying of the cross.

> **"And anyone who does not take his cross and follow me is not worthy of me."**
> MATTHEW 10:38

Every believer must be loyal first to God above any other relationship; they must be committed and willing to suffer for him and his cause, even unto death. Sadly, one of the greatest tragedies of the Christian experience is Christians who would gladly die for Christ but are not willing to live for him. It's as if they are saying, "Lord, I would rather die than give you more of my time, I would rather die than quit my great-paying job to work in the ministry, I would rather die than give up my ambition, I would rather die than forgive my neighbor, I would rather die than do all the things that you're asking of me." Are you carrying your cross? If not, what is it that is keeping you from it? For when we carry our cross and cease to make pleasing ourselves the goal of our life, we become free. Life begins to take on the flavor of what it was really meant to be. Is Christ really the Lord of your life?

THE
CIRCLE

Christ invites you today to take up your cross and live.

God, life can be so hard sometimes. My cross gets really heavy and all I want to do is just lay it down. Please give me the strength to keep holding on even when the road gets rough. Amen.

WAIT AND LISTEN

Hearing. Listening. As you've no doubt already learned, these two words are not synonyms for one another. There is a distinct difference between them. While hearing stops at the ears, listening goes all the way to the brain, to the heart. How many times have you been listening to a sermon or been in the midst of a conversation and found your mind wandering down a rabbit trail based on something you just heard? You may be hearing them, in the strict sense of being aware of their speaking, but you certainly aren't listening to them. You have no idea what they're saying; it isn't penetrating your ears and sinking into your brain and heart. Those are occupied with other thoughts.

> **God keeps renewing the promise and setting the
> date as *today*, just as he did in David's psalm,
> centuries later than the original invitation:
> Today, please listen, don't turn a deaf ear...**
> HEBREWS 4:7 (MSG)

God has invited us to listen to him, not just to hear him.
He knows there's a temptation to hear what he has to say
without really listening to it. Because listening to it means
we have to act on it, and acting on it
means we have responsibility, and
that's maybe a little more than we
really want at this time in our lives.
Still, his invitation to listen stands.
And the wonderful things we discover
when we take him up on it. Amazing
things. The God of the universe is
imploring us to listen to what he has
to say, he's pleading with us not to turn a deaf ear to him.
What he has to say will change the world—and our lives—
if we listen.

THE
CIRCLE

God's invited you to listen to what he has to say. Are your
ears turned toward him?

*God, I can't imagine turning a deaf ear to you.
That blows my mind. I'm even more awed that
you're asking me to listen to you. But I do listen.
I want to hear you. I want to listen to you.
I want to know what you think about everything, God. Thanks for bringing me into the
loop. I love you, God. Amen.*

A LIFE OF FAITH

Remember how, when you were a child, you answered the question "What do you want to be when you grow up?" Thirty years later, you wonder what happened to that little girl or boy. Somewhere between triumph and failure, hope and discouragement, you decided to put away what you now call your "childish" dream. And because of a regular inability to reach the ideal, you have become quite content with the practical. Instead of having a passionate marriage filled with many "date nights," you have settled for an occasional night on the couch in front of the TV. Instead of a close-knit family that prays together, you have settled for one that speaks to one another only in times of crisis. Instead of being an active member of your church, you have settled for pew-warming and superficial relationships.

Then he touched their eyes and said,
"According to your faith will it be done to you."
MATTHEW 9:29

Many Christians live in this place of paralyzing drabness, forgetting that God desires that they have a fulfilling life. In the same way that Christ was willing to heal the blind man, he is also willing to heal your life. God wants you to have a passionate marriage, a praying family, and a sense of belonging within a thriving church. It's all yours on one condition: believe it. Unfortunately, most of the time we quit before we receive what we desire. In what areas of your life is your faith failing? It is God's most holy desire that his children become all they can be, and it breaks his heart when we settle for less. Do you believe that God can right the vexing issues of your life? According to your faith will it be done for you.

THE
CIRCLE

BELIEVE

God invites you to believe; all things are possible.

God, I believe. Please help my unbelief. Amen.

THE GIFT OF POWER

If you've ever gotten sucked into televised coverage of the Olympic Games, you've probably seen super-sized, muscle-bound weightlifters testing their strength, lifting hundreds of pounds at a time. You've probably seen toned, lithe sprinters tearing down the track. You've probably seen ripped gymnasts flying through the air, balancing their bodies in positions so difficult that it hurts just to watch. Athletes like these communicate a sense of power just by walking past you, but when they spring into action their performance is truly impressive. Eventually, however, these people will age and their physical strength will fade. Jesus offers us, his children, a power that will last the test of eternity: his own.

> **"Heal the sick, raise the dead, cleanse those who have leprosy, drive out demons. Freely you have received, freely give."**
> MATTHEW 10:8

Today's passage of Scripture is a portion of a commission Jesus gave to his disciples. He was telling them what they needed to do when they went about sharing the gospel, and part of this was giving of what they'd freely received from him. Jesus has given us a gift: the gift of his power. And while he healed the sick, and raised the dead, and cleansed the lepers, and drove out demons, he didn't do those things just to do those things. He did them out of love. Love for people. He couldn't stand to see people in bondage; that's how much he loved them. And he's given us the ability to have that kind of love. It is up to us, however, to share it with the world.

THE
OCTAGON

POWER

Jesus is inviting you to share his power. You've received it freely; will you give it freely as well?

Jesus, thanks for thinking of me. Thanks for using me as a conduit of your power. Especially the power of your love. Help me to love others the way you loved them. And in whatever way they need to see your love, let me love them that way. That's all I pray. Amen.

MINISTRY OF LOVE

He called them from their ordinary lives and trained them. Now he was sending them out to make their unique contribution to the vast work of the ministry. Sure, they still had many questions. Their teacher was an impossible act to follow; who could top raising someone from the dead? Yet because they had been given the power to do the same, they stepped out. We are here today because they did. What would happen if you decided to step out and do what God is telling you to do?

> **He called his twelve disciples to him and**
> **gave them authority to drive out evil spirits**
> **and to heal every disease and sickness.**
> MATTHEW 10:1

In our hierarchical society, by some unspoken code, we understand that being a lawyer is better than being a bank teller and being a doctor is better than being a high school teacher and so on. With such an artificial measuring rod, little wonder why we are constantly comparing ourselves to others! Do you believe that had you been smarter, sterner and more outgoing, you would be a more effective believer?

God does not pressure us to perform like others; instead he gives each of us the ability to do the things he wants us to do. It is interesting that when Christ chose his apostles, he picked an assortment of personalities with a mishmash of backgrounds, ranging from doctor to tax collector to fisherman. Perhaps it was because he understood that ministry involves more than preaching fiery sermons; for some it involves encouraging a distressed coworker or simply walking their elderly neighbor's dog. All these acts are ultimately intended to bring his love to the hurting. How is your ministry going?

THE HEPTAGON

REPRODUCTION

God's invitation says, "You have all you need. Go touch lives!"

God, I never really think of myself as a minister, but now I see how I too am called to do the work of the ministry. Thank you for giving me the ability to minister to the needs of the people you place in my path. Please give me the boldness to do it. Amen.

KNOCK, KNOCK

There's something about a knock at the door. It's so hard not to answer. We think, "Who's here to see me? This is unexpected." Or perhaps it has to do with all those shows and commercials we've seen where the camera crew and smiling host surprise someone at the door with an oversized check or some other life-changing prize. Whatever it is, it's difficult to resist answering a knock at the door. Jesus himself said he's standing at the door. Not the physical doors of our homes, but at the doors of our souls. Our hearts. He knocks.

Here I am! I stand at the door and knock. If anyone hears my voice and opens the door, I will come in and eat with him, and he with me.

REVELATION 3:20

Jesus is a gentleman. He has not brought the police with him, and he is not there to serve a warrant. There is no battering ram in sight. He will not pick the lock, nor will he go in through the window. If we don't want him in our hearts, he will respect that. He won't like it, because he loves us too much, but he respects our decision. So he knocks. And he waits for the invitation. We've talked so much about all the invitations Jesus extends to us, but there is an invitation we must extend to him. We must answer the door. We must open it wide. We must invite him in. He is the best houseguest one could ever hope for. We don't need to clean up the house for him. We just need to respond to his knock. He'll take care of the rest.

Jesus is knocking. Will you invite him in?

THE
HEXAGON

THE
FATHER'S
CHARACTER

Jesus, I hear your voice. I hear your knock. I swing wide the door, Jesus, and say, "Come in." Please, make yourself at home in me. Mold me. Shape me. Turn me into exactly what you want me to be. I give you the control, Jesus. You and you alone. I love you. Amen.

TIME TO BE COUNTED

I ntolerant. Fundamentalist. Bigot. These are negative
words that are not only non-complimentary, they also
carry heavy contempt. Incidentally, they also happen to be
the persecutor's choice words for describing people who take
a stand for what they believe.

> **"Do not be afraid of those who kill the body but
> cannot kill the soul. Rather, be afraid of the One who
> can destroy both soul and body in hell. Are not two
> sparrows sold for a penny? Yet not one of them
> will fall to the ground apart from the will of your
> Father. And even the very hairs of your head are all
> numbered. So don't be afraid; you are
> worth more than many sparrows."**
>
> MATTHEW 10:28-31

All human beings desire to be accepted. So when we walk
into the break room at work and hear people saying things
that are contrary to what we know to be true, we somehow
find a way to blend in with the surroundings. Sometimes we
just sit and listen, at other times we might actually smile or
laugh along. Then, when we leave we feel a little bit of that
indigestion Peter felt when he denied his Lord. Have you

been there lately? Christ tells us in advance that we will be persecuted. He also tells us not to be afraid. After all, what could your coworkers really do to you if you told them that you disagreed with what they were saying? What is the worst that could happen? A story is told of an old man who in his final breaths looked upward and began to tremble. When asked why he trembled, he muttered that he feared that he was about to enter the presence of the eternal King; not just any king, but One who had the power to kill both his body and soul, how he wished he were entering the presence of an earthly king. These are the thoughts of one who knows the fear of God. Be bold in your stand for Christ and know that the only person worth fearing is on your side.

THE
HEXAGON

THE
FATHER'S
PROTECTION

God's invitation to you says, "Stand up and be counted. What is the worst that could happen?"

God, persecution is never easy. Now, I realize that it is just part of the life of a believer and I ask that you would help me to just accept it and not be so afraid of the pain it brings. Help me to remember, Lord, that it is really my honor to go through it for your sake. Amen.

Additional copies of this and other Honor products
are available wherever good books are sold.

Other titles in this series:
God's Answer to Your Deepest Longings
A Passionate Life Devotional Journal

If you have enjoyed this book,
or if it has had an impact on your life,
we would like to hear from you.

Please contact us at:
Honor Books
Cook Communications Ministries, Dept. 201
4050 Lee Vance View
Colorado Springs, CO 80918

Or visit our Web site:
www.cookministries.com

HONOR **HB** BOOKS
Inspiration and Motivation for the Seasons of Life